Country

HEART & SOUL

EDITORIAL

VICE PRESIDENT/EDITOR-IN-CHIEF
Catherine Cassidy

EXECUTIVE EDITOR
Heather Lamb

CREATIVE DIRECTOR
Sharon K. Nelson

EDITORIAL SERVICES MANAGER
Kerri Balliet

PROJECT EDITOR
Marija Potkonjak

ART DIRECTOR
Scott Schiller

EDITOR/COUNTRY
Robin Hoffman

ASSOCIATE EDITOR/COUNTRY
Lori Vanover

EDITORIAL ASSISTANT/COUNTRY
Lorie L. West

COPY CHIEF
Deb Warlaumont Mulvey

COPY EDITORS
Dulcie Shoener
Joanne Weintraub

PROJECT PROOFREADER
Marybeth Jacobson

PHOTO COORDINATOR
Trudi Bellin

ASSISTANT PHOTO COORDINATOR
Mary Ann Koebernik

PRODUCTION MANAGER
Dena Ahlers

LAYOUT DESIGNER
Julianne Schnuck

BUSINESS

ASSOCIATE PUBLISHER
Chris Dolan

NEW YORK Greg Messina, John Dyckman, Sabrina Ng
nysales@rd.com

CHICAGO Monica Thomas Kamradt, Carl Benson
nysales@rd.com

WEST COAST Catherine Marcussen, *nysales@rd.com*

CLASSIFIEDS M. I. Integrated Media, Alycia Isabelle
brenda@mi-ms.com

CORPORATE INTEGRATED SALES DIRECTOR
Steve Sottile

VICE PRESIDENT, DIGITAL SALES AND DEVELOPMENT
Dan Meehan

DIGITAL/INTEGRATED DIRECTOR
Kelly Paxson

EXECUTIVE DIRECTOR, BRAND MARKETING
Leah West

VICE PRESIDENT, CREATIVE DIRECTOR
Paul Livornese

MARKETING MANAGER
Katie Gaon Wilson

VICE PRESIDENT/BOOK MARKETING
Dan Fink

VICE PRESIDENT/MAGAZINE MARKETING
Dave Fiegel

READER'S DIGEST NORTH AMERICA

PRESIDENT
Dan Lagani

PRESIDENT, CANADA
Tony Cioffi

PRESIDENT, BOOKS AND HOME ENTERTAINMENT
Harold Clarke

CHIEF FINANCIAL OFFICER
Howard Halligan

VICE PRESIDENT, GENERAL MANAGER, READER'S DIGEST MEDIA
Marilynn Jacobs

CHIEF MARKETING OFFICER
Renee Jordan

VICE PRESIDENT, CHIEF SALES OFFICER
Mark Josephson

VICE PRESIDENT, GENERAL MANAGER, RD MILWAUKEE
Lisa Karpinski

VICE PRESIDENT, CHIEF STRATEGY OFFICER
Jacqueline Majers Lachman

VICE PRESIDENT, MARKETING AND CREATIVE SERVICES
Elizabeth Tighe

VICE PRESIDENT, CHIEF CONTENT OFFICER
Liz Vaccariello

THE READER'S DIGEST ASSOCIATION, INC.

PRESIDENT AND CHIEF EXECUTIVE OFFICER
Robert E. Guth

International Standard Book Number (10):
1-61765-060-9
International Standard Book Number (13):
978-1-61765-060-4

Library of Congress Control Number: 2011942233

All rights reserved. Printed U.S.A.

FOR QUESTIONS OR TO ORDER ADDITIONAL COPIES:
Call toll-free: 800-880-3012

Visit: *shoptasteofhome.com/country* or *country-magazine.com*

© 2012 Reiman Media Group, LLC
5400 S. 60th St., Greendale WI 53129-1404

Cover: String Lake, Grand Teton National Park, Wyoming.
PHOTO BY TIM FITZHARRIS

Front pages: Barn in fog, Hood River, Oregon.
PHOTO BY STEVE TERRILL

Previous page: Rainbow over windmill, Kalispell, Montana.
PHOTO BY CHUCK HANEY

Back pages: Cape Neddick Lighthouse, York, Maine.
PHOTO BY CHUCK HANEY

*"When I go out into the countryside and see
the sun and the green and everything flowering,
I say to myself, 'Yes indeed, all that belongs to me!'"*

HENRI ROUSSEAU

A meadow of wildflowers in the San Juan Mountains, Colorado. PHOTO BY MARY LIZ AUSTIN

Dawn's first light casts a warm glow on farm fields in Peacham, Vermont. PHOTO BY WILLIAM H. JOHNSON

Welcome

I'VE ALWAYS LOVED this photo. It reminds me of a little valley on the eastern side of the New Munster Marsh in Wisconsin where the fog pools on cool, spring mornings.

I drive through there every day on my way to work, and I try to take a moment to enjoy the scene, no matter how tired or distracted I am. Sometimes the mist covers the valley like a soft, white ocean dotted with islands of trees and barns. Sometimes it floats high above the ground in ghostly layers. It always reminds me how lucky we are to live in a world of ever-changing wonder.

Magic moments like these fill our lives like stars in a velvety night sky. Some burst with joy, like an armful of flop-eared puppy. Others bring peace, like a kitten purring on your lap. Sometimes they inspire us to try harder. Sometimes they help us gratefully accept what we have.

For 25 years, *Country*'s readers and photographers have shared these moments in the pages of our magazine. Now we've put the best of those stories and photos in *Country Heart & Soul*.

So even when the stars seem lost in cloudy skies, the glare of city lights or a morning fog, open this book. You'll find them shining as brightly as ever.

Editor, *Country* magazine

Spring

Summer

Autumn

Winter

Spring
The Land Awakens

Lupines in the Tehachapi
Mountains, California.

I Love the Feel of Warm, Black Dirt

AFTER A LONG, COLD, dreary and somewhat housebound winter, I'm ever watchful for the first glimpse of spring.

How it thrills my heart to spy birds at my feeders after their long vacation in Southern climes, or the red tulips and yellow daffodils bravely poking through a lingering blanket of late-winter snow, or the new buds promising fragrant blooms on the lilac bushes that my husband's grandmother planted on our farm some 75 years ago.

What I miss most, though, during the frigid, frosty months, is my connection to the soil and what it produces, whether it's garden-fresh vegetables, sun-ripened fruits or brilliant blooms brightening my country landscape.

As strange as it may sound, I love the feel of warm, black dirt running through my fingers, the outdoorsy smell of fresh-turned dirt on my work clothes and, yes, even the taste of a morsel of dirt on my tongue.

In an almost spiritual way, dirt is the substance that ties me to the earth. Just as soil keeps plants firmly anchored, it also keeps me grounded in what's real and what's important.

Working with my hands—tilling soil, planting seeds, watering sprouts, hoeing weeds and harvesting crops—yields such a rewarding sense of accomplishment. The first day of spring, I dig my fingers deep into the soft earth. I can feel its energy, and my spirits soar.

**KAREN ANN BLAND
GOVE, KANSAS**

Rows of soybeans with farms in the distance, LaSalle County, Illinois. PHOTO BY TERRY DONNELLY

Draft horses share a tender moment while waiting to plow a field in Oneida, Tennessee. PHOTO BY PAT & CHUCK BLACKLEY

"He thought, 'Lord, please help me over that next ridge. Give me one more step, then one more after that.'"

You Can't Keep a Good Team Down

LEROY HEAGY WAS 18 when he came in from the barn with a headache and nausea. His family thought he had "the grippe," but when paralysis seized the left side of his body, his mother called the doctor in a panic.

The local physician couldn't figure out what was wrong, so he called in a second doctor. In hushed tones, they told LeRoy's parents that their son had polio.

The next day, the health officer placed a quarantine sign on the house. He crudely said, "When he's dead, call me and I'll remove the sign," leaving LeRoy's mother in tears.

His father put a ladder up to the porch roof so LeRoy's friends could talk with him through the bedroom window. Gradually, though, LeRoy grew so delirious he couldn't visit.

After four weeks, the delirium subsided and his strength began to return. But the paralysis remained. He sat at the window, watching his brothers working and playing outside, and silently vowed, *I will walk again. I'll milk those cows and plow the fields.*

He kept hot compresses on his paralyzed leg and arm to keep the muscles limber. Every day he got out of bed and tried to walk a little farther than he had the day before.

Eventually, LeRoy persuaded his father to let him help spread manure. The elder man rigged up a seat on the horse-drawn spreader, and LeRoy spent hours pushing manure off that wagon. Slowly, he regained the use of his arm with all that exercise.

Then one day, LeRoy talked his father into letting him plow behind the team. With his parents watching from the kitchen window, he took a step with his right foot and dragged the left one forward to take the next step.

He was oh so careful to make sure the horses went slowly, so he wouldn't fall. Every muscle in his body ached with the effort, and sweat poured down his forehead. He feared he might fall.

LeRoy couldn't let his parents see that, because they might make him stop. He thought, *Lord, please help me over that next ridge. Give me one more step, then one more after that.*

LeRoy didn't dare look up; he just kept focusing on that next step and the next one after that. Then he was there, on top of the ridge and headed downhill. When he finally glanced back and saw that he was out of sight of the house, he stopped the team and fell to the ground. Exhausted, he lay there feeling the soil beneath his hands and the sun on his face.

Then he noticed the pain in his legs, smiled and thanked God again. For months, there hadn't been any feeling at all. He rested a few minutes before pulling himself up, cracking the lines and getting back to work.

LeRoy Heagy was my grandfather. He married, raised a family and operated a dairy farm for 25 years with only a slight limp to remind us that determination—and a good team—can overcome almost any obstacle.

JANET STEWART
LEBANON, PENNSYLVANIA

The Amish Way

The Amish may seem like a people quaintly lost in time. But when you get to know them, you find they're regular folks searching for a way to keep close, loving relationships with God, family and community. They don't claim it's the best way. It's just their way.

Neighbor helps neighbor at an Amish barn raising. PHOTO BY DOYLE YODER

A Belgian team at work, Nippenose Valley, Pennsylvania. PHOTO BY TERRY WILD

Two Amish boys are all smiles at a sale (below). An early-morning ride along a country lane, Holmes County, Ohio (bottom).

PHOTOS BY DOYLE YODER

"When our preacher preached, he worked up a powerful appetite. And he took it out on Granddaddy's chickens whenever he got the chance."

Granddaddy's Gospel Birds

FRIED CHICKEN runs in my blood. We enjoyed its greasy country goodness every chance we got, especially on Sundays, when the whole family gathered for a hearty dinner at Grandmama and Granddaddy Thompson's house.

I suppose that's why they called it the gospel bird. But in our family, we had an even better reason. Every Sunday after church, the preacher, his wife and children joined us. That caused Granddaddy a certain amount of concern.

You see, when our preacher preached, he worked up a powerful appetite. And he took it out on Granddaddy's chickens whenever he got the chance.

One Sunday after the preacher and his family had stripped every chicken bone on the place squeaky clean, Granddaddy told me, his old rooster started strutting around the yard. Then it flew up onto the windowsill and let out the loudest, proudest crow they ever heard.

Startled and a little annoyed, the preacher wailed, "Brother David, what's going on with that rooster?"

Granddaddy smiled and said, "I guess you'd crow, too, if you'd just put five young 'uns in the ministry."

But that wasn't even Granddaddy's favorite chicken tale. He recalled that one summer day the preacher dropped by and asked for a drink of water.

It did get awfully hot traveling those dusty dirt roads on horseback, and Granddaddy's well was renowned for the refreshing coolness of its water. My daddy, Homer, pulled up a bucket and handed a dipperful to the thirsty preacher.

Well, the shocking coldness of that water took the preacher's breath away. As he gagged and coughed, his false teeth flew out of his mouth and down into the well. A soft "plunk" echoed up as they hit the water.

Unqualified disaster though it was, Granddaddy admitted he felt a twinge of guilty joy. Grandmama was frying chicken for supper, and it now looked pretty safe.

My loving, Christian Grandmama Bernice, however, failed to see the humor in her minister's predicament. So she went to her bedroom, knelt down and prayed, knowing that God would provide an answer.

Sure enough, she returned minutes later with a plan.

"Homer, run to the barn, fetch me a roll of baling twine and meet me at the well," she ordered.

With the glum, toothless preacher watching, she tied one end of the twine to a piping-hot, crispy, fried chicken leg and lowered it into the well. Down it sank until it reached the bottom.

The preacher's false teeth clamped onto that chicken leg like a starving catfish. And Grandmama Bernice pulled the teeth up slick as a whistle.

Everyone leapt for joy and praised God—except Granddaddy, of course. He was going to bed a little hungrier than he'd have liked that night.

REV. JERRY C. THOMPSON
GOOSE CREEK, SOUTH CAROLINA

Christ Church Episcopal in Rugby, Tennessee. PHOTO BY PAT & CHUCK BLACKLEY

Life Begins Anew...

Lambs nuzzle in a field in Marion County, Oregon.
PHOTO BY STEVE TERRILL

A meadow of lupines and penstemons, Mount St. Helens National Volcanic Monument, Washington. PHOTO BY TERRY DONNELLY

Camas Prairie Centennial Marsh, Camas County, Idaho. PHOTO BY TERRY DONNELLY

"Every spring is the only spring — a perpetual astonishment."

ELLIS PETERS

Baby red foxes peek out of their forest den. PHOTO BY TIM FITZHARRIS

"Now I understood why he chose the hens by clucking at them; he was looking for the talkative ones."

A Cluck a Day Keeps the Doctor Away

EVERY TIME BOB STOPPED in my office, he had something to complain about. A gifted and articulate grumbler, he never had a good word to say or a smile on his face.

Bob was an old New Mexico rancher who was clearly unhappy to now be living in town. And while he was hardly cheerful when I first met him, his mood seemed to darken more as the months went by. I dreaded his visits.

Late one spring, I realized my family had more chickens than we needed. So I hung a sign in the office that read, "Laying Hens for Sale." And who do you suppose was my buyer? It was Bob!

He looked over my Barred Rock hens very carefully and picked out six, using criteria I didn't understand. Usually, you might pick a hen by the color of her comb, the brightness in her eyes, the sheen of her feathers and the condition of her vent.

Bob picked them up and clucked at them. I didn't dare ask him, since I was sure to get a sharp answer.

A few months later, Bob stopped in the office again and he was smiling. Everyone stopped what they were doing and stared at him as he whistled his way back to my office. Bob handed me an angel food cake he'd made with eggs from his new hens. Then he told me a story that explained his demeanor.

Bob's wife was ill. They tried every medical facility within 200 miles of their ranch. Finally, they moved to Payson, Arizona, where they could be a couple of hours from the doctors in Phoenix.

His wife was giving up; she had lost her desire to eat or go outside and didn't feel like talking to anyone, including Bob.

They were high school sweethearts and still deeply in love after 50 years of marriage. Bob was afraid of losing her.

Now, a rancher becomes accustomed to making things work by the strength of his hands and the force of his will, but Bob was powerless to make her well.

Then he remembered how fondly she talked about the hens on her childhood farm.

Soon after he came home with the hens he bought from me, he found his wife sitting in the backyard. A hen was standing on the picnic table in front of her, and they were deep in a bilingual discussion—English and Plymouth Barred Rock.

It was the first time Bob's wife had laughed in a couple of years, and he was overjoyed. Now I understood why he chose the hens by clucking at them; he was looking for the talkative ones.

It may have been the better medical care or a better outlook, or both, but she started to improve. She had her breakfast outside each day with her chickens and laughed at how they bickered over her leftover toast.

I should have looked harder at why Bob was so bitter, rather than just dreading his visits. Serendipity provided an answer I never would have guessed. As for Bob, he found fewer things to complain about. The love of his life was back.

PATRICIA ILES
PAYSON, ARIZONA

Barred Rock rooster. PHOTO BY TERRY WILD

Farm-fresh eggs, Toy Cow Creamery,
Nippenose Valley, Pennsylvania (below).
Madeline makes a new friend (bottom).
PHOTOS BY TERRY WILD

After the Rain...

Mexican gold poppies, Harquahala Valley, Arizona (top). Marsh marigold, Ice Lake Basin, San Juan National Forest, Colorado (above).

PHOTOS BY LARRY ULRICH

Two rainbows are the perfect ending to a rainy day in Owens Valley, California. PHOTO BY LONDIE GARCIA PADELSKY

"Let the rain kiss you. Let the rain beat upon your head with silver liquid drops. Let the rain sing you a lullaby."

LANGSTON HUGHES

Storm clouds transform the desert sky over Monument Valley, Utah-Arizona border. PHOTO BY ROBERT DAWSON

Black Angus cow and her calf bond in a grassy pasture in San Luis Obispo, California. PHOTO BY LONDIE GARCIA PADELSKY

*"We put the tiny, shivering orphan into
the trailer with Blaze and held our breaths."*

A Calf Named Bittersweet

MY DAY STARTED at 4:10 a.m. with devastating news. Blaze, my favorite cow, had delivered a stillborn calf.

When my husband, Cary, told me the news, I burst into tears. I've raised cattle all my life, but I'm still not immune to these everyday farm tragedies. I guess I never will be.

We gave Blaze a checkup and discovered she had a nasty infection. I knew that the infection wasn't the only reason she seemed so sad and listless.

The next day, I walked out to the pasture and found her licking a newborn black calf! She must've had twins!

Elated, I ran down the hill, only to find another cow named Red Wave vying for the calf's attention. This first-time mom showed signs of recently calving, so I knew the calf was hers.

I felt so bad for Blaze, but had to lead her away so she wouldn't keep Red Wave from nurturing her calf.

The next day, Blaze didn't show up for her evening feeding. This was alarming, since she is a very tame, former show heifer who's always ready to eat. So, we set out to find her with Rory, our trusty Australian shepherd dog, leading the way.

As the setting sun's dying rays glistened off the creek, we trudged through damp woods past chattering birds and a small herd of deer. Finally, on a vine-covered hillside, we spotted a white blaze on a black face peeking through the underbrush.

Leaving Cary and Rory, I worked my way through the tangled vines and sat down beside my old friend. I stroked her neck, and she laid her head in my lap. We sat sharing our sorrow, until the failing light and Cary's waning patience forced us to head home.

Later that evening, Cary and I were watching a movie when the phone rang. Cary answered and I heard the alarm in his voice as he said, "I'll be right over." Figuring someone was having calving problems, I simply asked, "Who?"

Our neighbor had a cow struggling to deliver twins. Cary said he'd be back soon. I knew better, though, and went to bed.

The next morning, our neighbor called again. He and Cary had successfully brought the twins into the world, but their mother didn't make it. Cary immediately volunteered to take one of the orphan calves.

We loaded Blaze into a trailer and drove to the neighbor's house. Then we put the tiny, shivering calf into the trailer with Blaze and held our breaths.

It didn't look good. Blaze sniffed at the little orphan, but stood back. The calf tentatively approached this strange cow, then lost courage and wobbled to the far corner of the trailer.

Then it happened. The calf managed a weak little squeak of a moo, and Blaze answered with the soft, easy low of a mama cow. That's all it took. Blaze and her adopted baby are now as bonded as can be. We named the little heifer Bittersweet.

As I sit on the hillside above the pasture watching all our pairs grazing, I'm reminded why I love living in the country. It's so alive and ever-changing, blessing us with sorrow followed by joy, death followed by life. My life on this land is a precious gift. And with it, I am truly contented.

SARAH AUBREY
ELWOOD, INDIANA

Breath of Spring Air...

View from the Appalachian Trail, Shenandoah National Park, Virginia.
PHOTO BY PAT & CHUCK BLACKLEY

Ice plants bloom on the cliffs above Big Sur, California. PHOTO BY TIM FITZHARRIS

Mount McKinley in Denali National Park & Preserve, Alaska. PHOTO BY DAVID SHAW

"Although we made messes constantly, I don't remember my parents ever complaining. We were farm kids, and they encouraged us to get outside and be adventurous."

Kids Can Be Kids in the Country

AS SPRING GRADUALLY CREPT in last year, my yard became a treasure trove of items the snow had been hiding.

Over there, in the sandpile, was a set of plastic measuring cups I'd been looking for. In my flower bed I found an antique serving spoon I had picked up at a garage sale, and under the deck was the bath towel I'd long since given up hope of finding.

No, I'm not usually this unorganized. It's my kids. Although my 17-year-old is past the stage of dragging half the house into the yard, my 13- and 11-year-old sons are not immune to it. When they've got a project in mind, nothing in the house is sacred.

Starting a fort behind Dad's shop? No problem. It will take a lot of nails, hammers, pieces of sheet metal and snacks, lots of snacks. That's why I found so many cups and plastic glasses out there behind the shop.

A go-cart racetrack? OK. It's going to take lots of poster board to make signs and some scrap fabric for flags. That explains why my good scissors were lying abandoned on the track.

A new puppy? Of course, it will need food and water bowls, and my mixing bowls will do the trick. They were old anyway, weren't they, Mom?

I have to confess that my sons get it from me. My younger sister, brother and I grew up on a farm and had endless creative projects and ideas that must have driven our mom crazy.

I well remember the perfume project, where we were going to bottle and market a scent that would make millions. We gathered every container in the house and proceeded to mix together talcum powder, bubble bath, perfume—whatever we could find.

Another time we set out to create the perfect cake recipe. We stirred together flour, eggs, sugar, all in vastly uneven proportions, and baked it. It was thin and hard and resembled pancakes. We threw it over the fence to the hogs.

Then there was the haunted house in the barn. As high school students, we had planned a slumber party for our friends, and a haunted house in the barn would be the perfect frightening way to end the evening. We spent weeks in the haymow stringing extension cords, hauling up old pieces of furniture and hammering together signs.

When I was home a year or so ago, there were still traces of that haunted house in the barn. And I complain that my kids don't put things away!

Although we made messes constantly, I don't remember my parents ever complaining. We were farm kids, and they encouraged us to get outside and be adventurous.

I'm trying hard to be that way, too. I really am. I won't even groan the next time the boys ask to use the spaghetti strainer to catch minnows in the creek.

VALERIE VAN KOOTEN
PELLA, IOWA

Lyla sniffs a darling bud of May in Avila Valley, California (top). A big, juicy mud puddle is a little boy's playground (above).
PHOTOS BY LONDIE GARCIA PADELSKY

Puppy kisses, San Luis Obispo, California. PHOTO BY LONDIE GARCIA PADELSKY

A 1953 Allis-Chalmers WD-45. PHOTO BY GARY ALAN NELSON

*"I happened to glance out the barn window and saw
my mother chasing the driverless tractor around in circles."*

The Fugitive Allis-Chalmers

MY FATHER WAS ALWAYS out working on our farm. Sometimes Dad got so busy in the field or the barn that he forgot about eating. This didn't sit well with my mother. Mom was the kind of woman who insisted people eat regularly.

You couldn't visit our home without having something to eat, no matter what time of the day or night you arrived. If your drive home was longer than a mile, she made bologna sandwiches just in case you got hungry on the way.

Food was important on the farm. We did a lot of hard, physical labor, the kind that gave us healthy appetites. So we ate a lot, and we ate often.

Once morning chores were done, we ate breakfast. Around midmorning, we'd have a bit more to eat. We called it lunch. At noon, we'd have dinner. In midafternoon, we would have a little lunch again, and after we finished the night milking, we'd have supper.

Nowadays, folks eat lunch when dinner used to be, and dinner in place of supper. Supper is something that's eaten at church. I don't know what to call our old midmorning and midafternoon lunches—going off your diet, I guess.

Mom knew the importance of eating on time, too. She worried about my father working so hard out in the field without proper nourishment. She solved that problem by taking meals out to him, along with a little for herself.

Depending upon whether it was lunch, dinner or supper, she might pack bologna sandwiches, sugar cookies or doughnuts in a brown paper bag. The bag always showed a stain left by escaping butter or mayonnaise. On occasion, Mom packed some potato salad or leftover meatloaf.

One day, I was doing the night milking while Dad finished cultivating a field behind the barn. We were all running late, so Mom made supper for Dad, placed it in a brown paper bag and started up our old Allis-Chalmers WC tractor to drive out to the field with his meal.

A short time later, I happened to glance out the barn window and saw my mother chasing the driverless tractor around in circles. I found out later that she had lost her balance and fallen off the tractor while checking to make sure she had packed Dad's potato salad. She had held onto the steering wheel as long as she possibly could, crimping it and causing the tractor to keep turning in small circles.

Removing the milkers from the cows, I ran out to the field where Mom was still pursuing the runaway tractor. I was able to jump up into the seat of that old iron horse and put a stop to its foolishness at last.

Once I stopped the fugitive Allis-Chalmers and saw that Mom was OK, I lectured her on her actions. I pointed out she could have been seriously injured.

"Why did you have to chase the tractor?" I asked.

"It had your father's potato salad," was her reply.

**AL BATT
HARTLAND, MINNESOTA**

Lush Landscapes...

Bald cypress forest, Lake Fausse Pointe State Park, Louisiana.
PHOTO BY TIM FITZHARRIS

Twin Falls cascades over limestone along the Caney Fork River in Rock Island State Park, Tennessee. PHOTO BY LARRY ULRICH

Horses graze in a field of buttercups in Sugar Hill, New Hampshire. PHOTO BY PAUL REZENDES

**Bigleaf maples along the Hall of Mosses Trail,
Olympic National Park, Washington.**

PHOTO BY TERRY DONNELLY

Summer
Season of Growth

The rocky shores of Davids Island, Vinalhaven, Maine.
PHOTO BY PAUL REZENDES

Never Ask a Rancher Why He Does What He Does

HARD WORK is synonymous with being a West Texas rancher. There are never enough hours in the day to accomplish what he has planned even though he may rise at 4:30 in the morning to get a head start on trucks coming to transport livestock to market or shearers arriving that day to shear his flocks.

He breathes the suffocating dust from the herd, the hot exhaust of the tractor and the chaff of grain and hay. He's the target of flying hooves, swishing tails, snorting nostrils and pointed horns and the victim of hailstorms, droughts, floods, high interest rates, low selling prices and a host of hungry insects.

Ask a rancher why he continues in the face of all this adversity, and he'll probably shift to the other foot and a slow, thoughtful smile will cross his weathered face. Chances are he's thinking of a wobbly calf he helped into the world only yesterday or the velvety nose of his favorite mare as she nuzzles her greeting.

He knows the overwhelming peace that comes from watching the sun rise and set on his little domain, and the wonder of being a part of God's divine plan of nature.

He treasures the freedom to walk through a meadow of wildflowers, sit by the creek, daydream from the porch or just rest on a bale of hay when he wishes. He lives by his own time clock—not someone else's.

He remembers the thankfulness he feels as the rain falls "just right" after a long dry spell, and the brilliance of a rainbow that arches across the sky as the clouds move on. Come bedtime, he is in awe of the oversize moon that turns the night into a molten silver landscape and feels privileged to see it.

His eyes light up proudly as he thinks of his wife, who is truly his helpmate in every way, and his children, who matured in the saddle or on the seat of a tractor.

So never ask a farmer or rancher why he keeps on keepin' on. Unless you've smelled the dampness of the soil or felt the kiss of a cool breeze on your face as it blows across your land, you really wouldn't understand his answer anyway.

MILDRED WICKSON
MENARD, TEXAS

"*All that we behold is full of blessings.*"
WILLIAM WORDSWORTH

With a lantern to guide him, this cowboy checks the herd at sunset in Washoe County, Nevada. PHOTO BY LONDIE GARCIA PADELSKY

A couple of buckaroos learn the cowboy trade near Stanford, Montana. PHOTO BY CHUCK HANEY

> *"Looking back, I can see now that Grandpa had more in mind than the roundup. He hoped we'd learn to love our animals and the land."*

Life Is a Cow Trail

THE TRAIL SEEMED safely exciting as I eased my horse along behind Dad, Grandpa and Paint, Grandpa's favorite horse. Surrounding me were brothers, uncles and hired hands who might as well have been uncles.

Everyone pitched in when it was time to round up the cattle. Even a kid like me.

My grandpa, Bill Eaton, built this ranch in the Yakima River Canyon near Ellensburg, Washington. He was not only the boss, but a trusted leader and decision-maker. He assigned jobs according to our abilities, and I had one just like every other hand.

It was hard work, sometimes wringing out tears of pain and frustration. But I never let on. When you're on the trail, you're a man. Being 7 years old had nothing to do with it. Like any other dependable hand, I tried my very best to do my job and do it well.

When you succeeded, Grandpa was quick to praise. He let you know he appreciated the effort, and you could tell he meant it. He was just as quick to tell you when you could do better. You knew where you stood with Grandpa.

Later, in the bunkhouse, the other ranch hands enjoyed a little good-humored laughter at my expense. For example, I had to rope a tight gate and pull it open with my horse because I could not budge it by hand.

They also kidded me about the ornery sore-footed bull I left behind in the brush because he kept fighting me off. And they just loved my classic seat-first landing after a sage grouse spooked my horse and tossed me.

I didn't mind—too much—because that's what cowhands do after a day's work. And I was a regular hand now.

Then one day, Grandpa wasn't leading the way. Dad rode all by himself up there ahead of the herd. And the work seemed a lot tougher. The new boss figured I could handle more work and more responsibility, now that I was a few years older.

With more responsibility came more mistakes. But just like Grandpa, Dad was willing to live with that. Someday it might be my turn to lead the ranch hands out onto the trail. He knew I needed to make my share of mistakes and learn from them.

Looking back on those times, I can see now that Grandpa had more in mind than the roundup. Sure, he needed to get those cattle in, but he was even more interested in helping shape our decision-making skills, sense of responsibility and respect for an honest day's work.

He encouraged us to appreciate the deer crossing the trail up ahead, the coyote pup tagging along behind, and even the sage grouse that once gave me such a wild ride and sore backside. He hoped we would learn to love our animals and the land.

Grandpa was trying to teach us that life is like that cow trail. It doesn't start at 8 or end at 5. It begins when it's light enough to see and ends when the job is done.

Just like the trail, life may seem safe and familiar sometimes, but it isn't. Accidents and mistakes take their toll. You do the best you can, and that's all you can do.

Every decision brings consequences, good and bad, regardless of intentions. Opportunities for scrapes and bruises lurk around every bend, along with the promise of rewards far greater than those measured in dollars and cents.

As I grew into a life of my own, I sometimes found myself wishing I could simply trail along with Grandpa and Paint forever, talking and enjoying the ranch as it spread out before us. Those were times I enjoyed with every fiber of my being.

But that wouldn't be real life, would it? I wouldn't have four wonderful children of my own, or four precious grandchildren. I wouldn't have earned the chance to discover that life isn't really about money or the things you can buy with it.

Our true, lasting legacies can't be bought, spent or lost. They're things like decision-making skills, a sense of responsibility and a heartfelt respect for all that God created. I hope my grandkids will remember their grandpa as I remember mine: for the lessons learned along the cow trail.

KEN EATON
PLAINS, MONTANA

The Way Out West

Before barbed wire and fences, the American cowboy freely roamed the frontier, moving cattle from ranch to rail. Today you will still find the cowboy working the Great Plains, the Rockies, the Sierras and anywhere else ranches thrive. It's a hard life, but one no cowboy or cowgirl would trade for a corner office.

A brewing storm doesn't stop a cattle roundup in the eastern Sierra Nevada. PHOTO BY LONDIE GARCIA PADELSKY

A cowgirl and faithful friend take a break in Owens Valley, California (top); mending fences is just part of the job (above).

PHOTOS BY LONDIE GARCIA PADELSKY

Riding and roping, Bighorn Mountains, Wyoming.

PHOTO BY JEFF VANUGA

> *"Look deep into nature, and then you will understand everything better."*
>
> ALBERT EINSTEIN

The Bryce Amphitheater at Bryce Canyon National Park, Utah. PHOTO BY TIM FITZHARRIS

His Guardian Angel

MY SON DOUG and his favorite horse, JB, spent countless happy hours on the trails around our farm in southeastern Idaho. They especially enjoyed roaming the nearby Teton Range with family and friends.

A big, beautiful quarter horse, JB seemed to love Doug every bit as much as Doug loved him.

During his first three years of college at Utah State University, in Logan, Doug spent his summers working on the farm and riding JB on weekends. After his third year—with just a few courses left to earn his degree in accounting—Doug decided to finish up in summer school.

One of Doug's friends even offered the use of a pasture near school, so he wouldn't have to spend the summer apart from JB. The week before school started, Doug loaded JB and another one of our horses into a trailer and headed for Logan.

With a second horse, Doug figured he wouldn't have to ride alone. His roommate and many of his friends were riders, and my husband planned to visit and explore some new trails in the beautiful Cache Valley and nearby mountains.

A few days later, Doug's roommate called and asked if I'd heard from him. Doug had gone riding alone the morning before. No one had seen him since, and no one knew where he'd gone.

My husband and I drove down to Utah and contacted the Cache County Sheriff. He organized a search and rescue posse. After that, all we could do was wait—and worry. It was one of the hardest days of our lives.

After searching all day, the sheriff was about to give up when they found our son. His body lay in a steep ravine in the foothills near Clarkston. They figured he tried to ride up out of the ravine, and JB had flipped over backward on top of him. His saddlebags held a full bottle of water and a sandwich for lunch, so Doug must've fallen early in his ride.

The man who found Doug said he spotted him only because he saw JB in the bottom of the ravine. Doug's horse had patiently stood beside his fallen friend for three hot days and two cold nights without food or water.

We were heartbroken and always will be. But we take some solace in knowing that our son died doing what he loved. And ever since that day, all of us have felt a special bond with JB.

When our son was missing, I prayed that God would send angels to watch over him until we could find him. Doug's angel was a quarter horse named JB.

ARLENE CANNON
SHELLEY, IDAHO

A mare nuzzles her newborn foal on a foggy morning in San Luis Obispo, California. PHOTO BY LONDIE GARCIA PADELSKY

The Land Blossoms...

Giant coreopsis, Point Arguello, Santa Barbara County, California.
PHOTO BY LARRY ULRICH

A field of purple coneflowers below Mount Adams, Klickitat County, Washington. PHOTO BY STEVE TERRILL

The center of a dahlia (top) and a yucca (above).

PHOTOS BY STEVE TERRILL

"I go to nature to be soothed and healed, and to have my senses put in order."

JOHN BURROUGHS

Prairie grass awaits a refreshing summer thunderstorm in Badlands National Park, South Dakota. PHOTO BY TIM FITZHARRIS

California poppies and lupines surround an oak tree in Stanislaus National Forest, California. PHOTO BY MARY LIZ AUSTIN

An Accidental Treasure

SEEMINGLY OUT OF PLACE, a solitary hickory tree towers above the corn on our farm.

The tree is a stately monument to George Ingram, a neighbor of my grandfather's who accidentally planted it sometime around the turn of the century.

The story goes that George was tending the field with his team of oxen when he heard the dinner bell ring. Hungry from the day's work, he took the newly cut hickory switch he was using to urge the oxen on and stuck it in the ground near a fencerow, then hurried home and forgot about it.

He never did retrieve the switch that day, and later found it rooted firmly in the rich soil. As it grew in stature, the tree became a favorite spot for George's children and grandchildren. And during the cold days of winter, the tree's nuts became a tasty addition to rich chocolate fudge, cookies and cakes.

Over the years, my aunt Loretta, who married George's son, Barney, saved the hickory tree from the saws and axes that cleared fencerows and removed all other trees in the field. Although the tree shades valuable cropland and takes water from the crops, it is a part of her heritage and the heritage of her children, grandchildren and generations to come.

I now live on my grandfather's farm, and I can stand on our back porch and admire the tree. A late-spring storm tore a large branch off it, but my cousin assured me that after the crop's out of the field, the branch will be removed, saving the tree. To me, the old hickory tree is a real treasure.

SHANNON MCKINNEY
HOLLAND, INDIANA

61

The Week I Fed the Banker's Pig

I WASN'T SURPRISED when my son, Jeff, a suit-wearing banker, announced he was going to raise a pig.

I had seen it coming. Our lineage is filled with Maine farmers (I'm not one of them), and to satisfy an ancestral yearning, Jeff bought a dilapidated 200-year-old farmhouse a year ago.

Lots of hard work went into fixing up the place, including the barn. After some months, he declared the barn fit for a pig. I couldn't disagree, but I certainly wasn't going to encourage it.

When the farm became home to a pig it was fine with me—I live six miles away. I thought that was a reasonably safe distance until the banker and his family decided to take a vacation and asked me to feed the animal on my way to work.

I reported for the first feeding early Monday morning. Jeff had carefully written instructions on two pages of a yellow legal pad—far more detailed than anything we ever left for his baby sitter. He left the food on top of the grain bin neatly portioned in plastic bags like individual microwave dinners.

In his pen, the pig was up on his hind legs, hanging what I would call his elbows over the top rail of the fence and watching me plod through the mud with an honest-to-goodness grin on his face. No mistake about it, he was enjoying my troubles.

I stuck out my tongue at him and dumped his breakfast into the feed trough. Then I replenished his water and left, taking care to fasten the gate.

At work a half hour later, the phone rang. The only sounds from the other end were a loud piglike snort and a giggle. It was the banker calling from somewhere on the road to make sure I'd remembered my chores. He hung up before I could express my current feelings about the joys of fatherhood.

I was a bit late reporting to the farm on Tuesday morning, and the pig was leaning over the fence—frowning. If he'd had a watch, he would have pointed at it.

The feeding was easy. Getting water was another matter.

Thus far, I had been able to tend to the pig without entering his pen. I found this a most agreeable method and had no intention of straying from it—even though the pig had pushed the watering pan well beyond my reach that morning. So I filled the bucket from the rain barrel and took careful aim at the pan.

Either the splash or a natural aversion to clean water startled the pig something awful and sent him spinning around the pen, throwing splatters of mud onto the front of my shirt. When I got to work, I took a sponge bath in the men's room.

Far left to right: Curious pigs in Shenandoah Valley, Virginia; kids compete in a greased pig contest in Churchville, Virginia; a pig snout. PHOTOS BY PAT & CHUCK BLACKLEY

It rained Tuesday night. By Wednesday morning, the ground in the pigpen, already the color of chocolate pudding, had achieved a consistency to match. Worse, the feeding trough was upside down, although still close enough to the fence that I could reach it. But the water pan had been shoved 3 feet farther to the back.

The pig had a smug look—his beady eyes wondered how I planned to get him water. I found a long stick and turned the feed trough right side up. It was on a bit of a slant, but good enough. I put the food in the top end of the trough and the water in the bottom. Now I was smug. The pig looked stumped.

On Thursday, the water pan was three-quarters buried and upside down on the far side of the pen. He must have been up all night burying it.

Maybe, I thought, both the pig and I could survive the one remaining day before the banker returned if I just added lots more water to his food. The heavily watered-down slop prompted a snooty sneer from the pig. I left for work anyway.

The sun blazed all day and my guilt rose with the temperature as I thought about the pig without fresh water.

When I finally drove up to the barn early Friday morning, I sighed in relief. Dehydrated pigs don't stand on their hind legs and lean over fence railings with disgusted looks on their faces.

It was a little embarrassing to realize how glad I was to see him, and I managed a warm hello. He ignored me.

Opening the pen door gingerly, I took a tentative squishy step toward the pig. He seemed a great deal bigger than he appeared from outside the rail. "Shoo," I said, trying to sound authoritative, but certainly not threatening. (It was sort of a loud "shoo" with a question mark after it.)

My shoes made a sucking sound as I approached the filthy trough. Carefully, with two fingers, I squeezed one end and ever so gently dragged it to the front of the pen.

The pig followed these proceedings closely and snorted encouragement. I'd have been happier if he had waited in the corner for me to get everything in order. But no, he had to lean against my legs as I retraced my steps to retrieve the water pan.

The rest was easy—clean water in the pan and fresh slop in the trough. The pig watched admiringly.

As I went around the corner of the barn, I looked back. The pig was slurping water like a sump pump. But he paused for a brief second to look up and smile. I felt a bit foolish, but I waved. I'm pretty sure that pig loves me.

EARL SMITH
BELGRADE LAKES, MAINE

All God's Creatures…

White peacock butterfly. PHOTO BY PAUL REZENDES

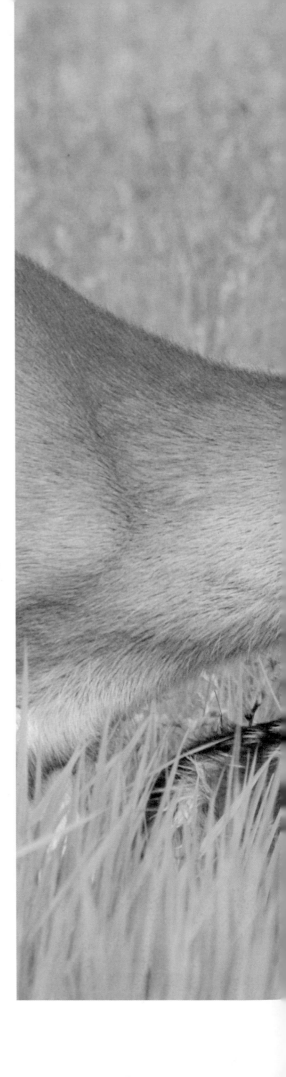

White-tailed doe and fawn, Shenandoah National Park, Virginia. PHOTO BY PAT & CHUCK BLACKLEY

A black bear cub and its mother, Pine County, Minnesota. PHOTO BY CATHY & GORDON ILLG

"Man's heart away from nature becomes hard."

CHIEF STANDING BEAR

Great egret, Everglades National Park, Florida. PHOTO BY PAUL REZENDES

"She knew that with the good Lord's help, she could provide a living for herself and her children."

Where There's a Will, There's a Way

MY MOTHER WAS BORN in 1894 in Mercer County, Kentucky. As the oldest of six children, she had to help care for her brothers and sisters, as their mother was not well.

In 1926, she married and eventually had six children of her own. Just before Christmas in 1940, her husband passed away. She would have to raise their children, ages 5 to 13, alone.

During the funeral, Mama overheard friends discussing her situation. They all agreed on one thing: The children would have to be put in an orphanage.

Mama silently vowed to do whatever it took to prevent that from happening. She knew that with the good Lord's help, she could provide a living for herself and the children.

She faced many problems. The 54-acre farm was not paid for, and the taxes were due. There were funeral expenses to pay, plus a small bill at the general store. And the children had to be clothed and fed. Mama tackled the problems one by one.

The Federal Land Bank was about to foreclose on the farm, so she went to Anderson National Bank and told her story. The kindhearted president loaned her $800 to pay off the other bank. She repaid Anderson National before her children were grown. (My sister Nancy and I still do business with that bank.)

Then there was the grocery bill. We owed $4.35 at Sam Stratton's store. Sam told my mother she could work off the debt by clearing some land for him with her three boys, who were then 9, 11 and 13. She was happy to do it. She never bought groceries on credit again.

Next came the funeral expenses. The funeral director said Mama could pay him in small amounts until the full bill was paid. She finally paid it off in 1947.

To feed and clothe us, she turned to the farm. In spring, the oldest boy, Rayford, hitched up the horses and began plowing to make a garden and grow some crops. This brought tears to Aunt Birdie's eyes. She cried for him because he was so young to take on so much responsibility.

We ordered some baby chickens by mail and kept them under a light for warmth around the clock. Soon we had eggs to sell and fried chicken to eat.

Mama bought two little pigs for meat. We fed them table scraps and a bit of corn. Sometimes we cut horseweeds to add to their feed. By butchering time, they weighed 200 or more pounds. We used every bit of the meat and rendered the fat for lard. Mama had turkeys, too, and sold them to other families at Thanksgiving and Christmas.

The neighbors could see that Mama was willing to work and was teaching her children to work. They began asking her to clean their houses, do laundry and work in the fields. She never refused a job, and she made sure all her children worked as well. She knew education was very important, too, and kept all her children in school for as long as they would go.

Mama's motto was, "Where there's a will, there's a way to do it." She believed in hard work, truthfulness and God. She left us a great heritage in the way she lived her life.

LYDA ROBINSON
SALVISA, KENTUCKY

Clothes on the line, Lycoming County, Pennsylvania (above). PHOTO BY TERRY WILD

Pet chickens, San Luis Obispo, California (top).
PHOTO BY LONDIE GARCIA PADELSKY

Picking lettuce in Greenville, Maine. PHOTO BY TERRY WILD

The Colorado River cuts through Dead Horse Point State Park in Utah. PHOTO BY TIM FITZHARRIS

*"With teary eyes, he proudly handed me
a fruit jar full of muddy water."*

The Gift of Life

YEARS AGO I LIVED IN northeastern Utah, a semiarid place where farmers carved homesteads out of sagebrush. In this part of the country, you had to buy water rights, and these small farmers could barely afford to get by. Most had large families and, for them, life was a constant struggle.

Some of these folks had never been out of the valley. They were very clannish and suspicious of outsiders like me. I had married into a family with 80 good acres.

To this day, I don't know how these folks knew I could find water with a forked stick. But word got around, and I helped whenever I could.

One day, an old pickup rattled into our yard amid a cloud of dust. An elderly man pushed several times on the rickety door before it opened.

He walked hesitantly up to me and swept his worn and weathered hat from his head and stood twisting it in his hands.

"I'm Fred Meeker and live way out in Frogtown," he said. "A friend told me you can find water with a stick. I don't have much of a water right and would like very much to have a little extra water for my stock and a few scraggly trees and shrubs the wife tries to make grow.

"We don't have much money, but when you get time, could you see if you can find any water on my place?"

I felt a deep compassion for hardworking farmers like him and replied, "If you can bring me back, I can go now and we'll see."

Fred got the old pickup running amid much sputtering and backfiring, and we took off. Conversation was impossible, so for most of the journey we were silent.

Upon arrival, we were met by a tired-looking, sweet-faced woman and a half dozen kids of various ages and sizes. The man told me he would feel blessed if water could be found in or near one of his corrals.

I took the forked branch from a willow tree I had cut before we left and held it upright in my hands. Then, I walked back and forth over the area, climbing in and out of several corrals.

Finally, the willow twisted down in my hands, and I centered the location from all directions. About 8 feet from the inside corner of the corral, I detected water.

Fred, who had followed me all the way, brought a big rock and placed it on the spot. He was obviously elated and kept pumping my hand in his enthusiasm. The kids were jumping up and down with excitement, and his wife was dabbing at the corners of her eyes with her apron.

She shyly offered me an old red baking powder can containing a few crumpled bills and some change.

I handed it back to her and delicately explained, "Thank you very much. I don't take payment for my efforts, as God has given me this talent as a gift, and I use it to help people."

I turned to Fred and said, "You will find water at 14 feet. It's surface water. Be very careful of cave-ins when you dig."

About a week later, the old pickup again rattled into our yard again. It was Fred. With teary eyes, he proudly handed me a fruit jar full of muddy water. No words were needed. The tears on his weathered face said it all.

SUNNY BARBER
APACHE JUNCTION, ARIZONA

71

Lighthouse Mystique

Long ago sailors braved the open sea with only the stars above and a faint light off an unknown shore to guide them to safety. Today lighthouses stand sentinel over the past, reminding us to preserve our history for future generations.

Heceta Head Lighthouse near Cape Creek, Oregon. PHOTO BY TERRY WILD

West Quoddy Head Lighthouse, Lubec, Maine (above). PHOTO BY STEVE TERRILL

Marquette Harbor Lighthouse, Lake Superior, Michigan (top). PHOTO BY LARRY ULRICH

Great Point Lighthouse, Nantucket National Wildlife Refuge, Nantucket, Massachusetts. PHOTO BY PAUL REZENDES

*"A little Southern lady was the life of that ol' place,
back when folks were neighbors the way God intended."*

My Neighbor's House

THE OTHER DAY, as I rounded the lazy curve before the crossroads below our house, a sunbeam broke through the clouds and lit up the old white farmhouse.

I'm part of a dying breed around here—what they call a local—and I've passed by here nearly every day of my life. But when that sunbeam hit the house, it took my breath away.

It had been left empty and at the mercy of the elements for many years. It's not like I never noticed how lonely the old place looked. I've heaved many a sad sigh as I drove past.

But this afternoon, the old gal was really showing her age, and it hurt me inside. Scrub trees had taken over the sloping yard, and wisteria shrouded what was left of the front porch and crawled across the stout lines of the rooftop and chimney.

For the first time, I felt as if the old house was dying. And then the memories flooded in, memories of when I was a carefree country boy and it was my neighbor's house.

A little Southern lady was the life of that ol' place, back when folks were neighbors the way God intended. She shared the bounty of her garden, her flowers and kind conversation on that very front porch. We worshipped in the same church, read the same local newspaper and lived the same simple lives.

We kids played barefoot in that front yard. It was the softest, finest grass I ever set foot on. We chased the lightning bugs around the roots of those old oaks and played hide-and-seek out back, under the shade of a lanky walnut tree.

In the summer, we ate homegrown watermelons and watched the cars go by from the front steps, while she and my mama sat in the swing and chattered on about the upcoming "protracting meeting." We waved at most of the folks passing by because we knew 'em! We waved even if we didn't know 'em.

I remembered the smells of tangy dried apples, canned peaches, sweet corn and fresh-cooked corn bread wafting from her kitchen through an open window.

I remembered tiny roosters cut from the sides of snuff cans that she had glued to the corners of an old pantry.

I remembered staring at the faces in family photos hanging along the shadowy hallway.

I remembered sitting stiffly in the straight-backed chair in her tiny bedroom when her time got short. I missed her. I missed her old-fashioned ways and the long-gone way of life she represented.

Everything moves so fast these days, busy as a cow's tail in July. It's too fast for me. And it's too fast for that old farmhouse. I hear they're planning to build a badly needed turn lane at the crossroads, right where the old farmhouse now stands.

I'll bet the folks who need that turn lane so badly never walked barefoot in that yard. Never got the thrill of seeing the wind toss golden-colored maple leaves down into that soft grass.

They never got acquainted with the little Southern lady who lived a simple, gracious life there or ate a slice of her corn bread. I did, though, and I'm forever grateful.

LARRY R. PIRKLE
DAWSONVILLE, GEORGIA

Wisteria adds beauty to an abandoned homestead in Camden County, Georgia. PHOTO BY PAUL REZENDES

Fruits of Our Labor...

Peaches, blackberries and raspberries. PHOTO BY TERRY WILD

Morning fog hovers over a field of round hay bales in Belgrade, Maine. PHOTO BY PAUL REZENDES

"God made the country,
and man made the town."

WILLIAM COWPER

Cows lazily graze on a lush green pasture in Jefferson, Maryland. PHOTO BY PAT & CHUCK BLACKLEY

Wheat glows in the setting sun. PHOTO BY TERRY WILD

An octagonal red barn and sweeping rows of corn, Pepin County, Wisconsin. PHOTO BY MARY LIZ AUSTIN

A country road, Judy Gap, West Virginia.
PHOTO BY PAT & CHUCK BLACKLEY

Autumn
Nature's Masterpiece

The Scent of Fall

STEPPING OUTDOORS one evening recently, I was greeted by the scent of fall in the cool, clean country air.

I knew autumn had arrived because the cattle had started to get their winter coats and our horse had lost his summer sheen. Flocks of Canada geese flew over our farm in precise formations, and the corn leaves whispered a song of maturity.

Almost overnight, the apples in our orchard turned red. I bit into one on the way in from feeding the horse. It tasted snappy, juicy and delicious.

A few weeks ago, our garden was green and lush. Now, it has that weathered look. There are only a few green tomatoes left on the vine to ripen. The grapes are ready to be picked, and the mums are budded and set for the last blast of color for another year.

These are all telltale signs of autumn. But the one I enjoy most is that special scent that lingers on a crisp, calm evening and is still there when I walk outside in the morning.

I can't describe it. I just know that when I get a whiff of it, summer is gone and fall is in the air.

DARWIN ANTHONY
TRIMONT, MINNESOTA

White birches stand out amid the fall foliage in Split Rock Lighthouse State Park, Minnesota. PHOTO BY TERRY DONNELLY

Apples ready to be picked in Welltown, Virginia. PHOTO BY PAT & CHUCK BLACKLEY

> *"Every so often we talk about taking out the stump and planting something else, but no other tree seems worthy of that spot."*

Love Grows on Trees

THE MASSIVE LOG BURNING in the fireplace fills the dining room with the fruity smell of apple wood.

One of the thick lower branches, it had been cut into chunks just small enough to fit into the firebox. That single log will sputter and crackle and spill out heat for the rest of the afternoon and into the evening.

The warmth, scent and cheerful sounds stir memories of a tree that was more than a tree. She was a faithful old friend.

Gnarled and twisted, the apple tree was already ancient when we moved into our house 25 years ago. Twigs and suckers sprouted willy-nilly among the bigger branches. To my knowledge, no one had ever pruned or sprayed her.

I imagine she stood sentinel in the yard when our home was a country schoolhouse. Kids nearly a century ago probably played under her and tasted her apples, kids who have grown old or long since passed on.

We didn't realize until we'd lived here for a few months that we were merely the tree's caretakers. Apparently, local cider makers vied for rights to the apples each fall. We didn't know these people, but they knew our tree well.

The family who came the first year—a group of grown brothers with several young children in tow—had a simple system. The smallest adult climbed to the top and jumped up and down on one of the larger branches.

The tree shook and apples rained down, plopping and bouncing into the grass. After he'd shaken all the branches, everyone scurried underneath to collect the harvest.

As our family grew, babies took their naps in the playpen we carried out into the shade of the tree on warm summer afternoons. Netting covered the top of the playpen to protect the little ones from the tiny green apples that dropped from branches through the summer.

As the kids grew older and played ball in the backyard, the old tree played, too, gobbling up their balls and hiding them in the hollow center of her trunk.

We knew we wouldn't have her much longer. The cavity in her trunk dropped almost to the roots. It happened in stages. The first section broke off a few years ago during a heavy snowstorm.

We talked of cutting her down. We knew it was just a matter of time, but didn't have the heart. So she stood there for a few more years, lopsided and gnarlier than ever.

Last fall's windstorm brought the final blow. The huge trunk split wide open to reveal crumbly black insides. One lone branch remained. I intended to tell our hired hand not to cut it off. But before I had a chance, his chain saw had severed the whole tree from the stump.

He didn't bother to split it, since most of the insides were rotten. He just piled the pieces in a heap to get them out of the way.

We salvaged a couple of the larger logs for our fireplace, and said goodbye to our old friend. Every so often, we talk about taking out the stump and planting something else, but no other tree seems worthy of that spot.

We still don't know what to do with our backyard, but I'm reminded of Shel Silverstein's *The Giving Tree*. Like the apple tree in his classic children's book, our old friend gave us everything she had to give.

And now, when it seems as if there's nothing left, she keeps on giving. We will always cherish her for that.

BARB RATHBUN
NAPLES, NEW YORK

"There were men from the sawmill, businessmen, secretaries...people from every walk of life. They came because they were overcome by the thought of what it would be like if the Pauls' tragedy were their own."

All's Well Here

IT'S HARVESTTIME AGAIN, and as I watch the spud trucks rumbling by and see the diggers and crossovers moving up and down the fields, my mind returns to an event that happened many years ago.

It was spud harvest, and school was out for two weeks. Everyone had lots to do. We were loading hay into our loft when the message came: Mrs. Paul and her children were in an accident while visiting relatives in Salt Lake City, and several of them were in critical condition.

Mr. Paul dropped everything and headed to the hospital, asking if we could feed his cattle while he was gone. But wasn't there more we could do? Dad said he'd handle my chores if I wanted to go. We knew they still had potatoes to dig, as well as late-season hay in the field. We didn't have potato equipment, but I knew I could work hay.

I loaded our hay piler onto our truck and headed out, wondering who would be driving for me. I needn't have worried. Cars, trucks, potato diggers and every other imaginable piece of equipment were heading to the Paul farm from every direction.

A real estate agent volunteered to drive as I stacked the bales coming up the side of the truck; other trucks poured onto the field. Shortly after dark, all the hay was safely in the barn. A group of men helped me feed the cows before we retired for the night.

At dawn the next day, I returned to take care of the animals. Again, I was not alone. I directed a whole crew with Mr. Paul's feeding instructions. After the sun warmed the air enough, the half dozen or so diggers again started rolling through the fields. I took the job of forking away the debris piling up along the edges of the conveyor belt in one of the cellars.

A banker stood on one side of me, a schoolteacher on the other. There were men from the sawmill, businessmen, secretaries, fellow teenagers, people from every walk of life. Some were rough characters, some were highly refined, but their hearts were much the same. Some didn't even know the Pauls. They came because they were overcome by the thought of what it would be like if the Pauls' tragedy were their own.

There were so many people and so much equipment that our biggest problem was just keeping out of one another's way. The potatoes were outpacing the cellars' capacity, and some diggers went on to other jobs. In short order, the harvest was in and the machinery went back to the farms from which it came. The farmers who'd brought it still had their own fields to harvest. They'd chosen to help a neighbor first.

Late that night, a small group of us were finishing up the feeding when we saw headlights coming up the driveway. Mr. Paul emerged and approached to thank us.

"How's the family?" someone asked him.

Mr. Paul looked down. "Not well," he said. "But some other relatives came so I could come home and try to get the harvest in."

A member of our group put a hand on Mr. Paul's shoulder. "Perhaps you should look in the cellar," he said.

As Mr. Paul stepped in and flipped the switch, shining the lights on huge mounds of potatoes, this tough man with work-roughened hands started to sob.

The kind neighbor again put a hand on his shoulder. "You go back to your family," he said gently. "All's well here."

More than 25 years later, I still see these acts of kindness occurring. And as long as I do, I know those words, embedded deep in my heart, will still ring true. All's well here.

DARIS HOWARD
ST. ANTHONY, IDAHO

Windrowed hay, Shenandoah Valley, Virginia. PHOTO BY PAT & CHUCK BLACKLEY

Bridges to the Past

If you should drive down a quiet country road, you might be blessed with the privilege of crossing a covered bridge. These beloved structures span not only creeks and rivers, but time itself. They are a symbol of a quieter age and a sign to slow down, take a deep breath of fresh, country air and enjoy the view.

Covered bridge over the Sunday River, Bethel, Maine. PHOTO BY STEVE TERRILL

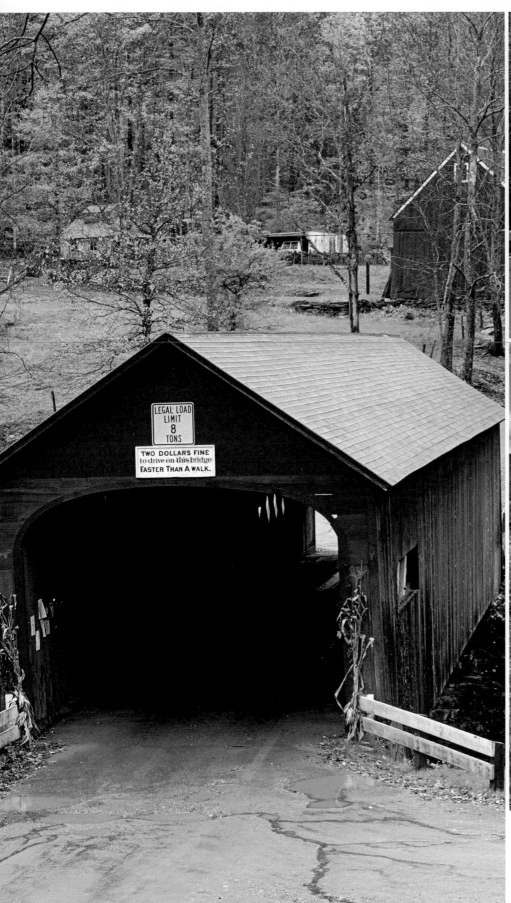

The Cedar Covered Bridge, Madison County, Iowa, was burned down in 2002 and rebuilt two years later (above).
PHOTO BY STEVE TERRILL

Bissell Covered Bridge, Charlemont, Massachusetts (top).
PHOTO BY PAUL REZENDES

Built in 1870, this bridge spans the Green River in Guilford, Vermont.
PHOTO BY TERRY DONNELLY

Fall envelops Shot Beech Ridge in Great Smoky Mountains National Park. PHOTO BY TERRY DONNELLY

"Red, orange and yellow leaves fall around me like a multicolored curtain. The mountains are beautiful in the light of day. A multitude of sights, smells and sounds overwhelms my senses."

On Top of the World

THERE IS NO PEACE quite like nighttime in the Smoky Mountains. Each fall, I make a pilgrimage to the summit of Laurel Mountain to find the serenity buried in my soul. Henry David Thoreau had his Walden Pond. Others have their bustling towns and bright city lights. I have my beloved Smoky Mountains.

The clear water of a rushing stream tumbles past me on its way through the valley. I follow its winding path around the base of the mountain.

Autumn daytime in the Smoky Mountains is alive with the sights and sounds of singing birds, buzzing insects and other wildlife. Red, orange and yellow leaves fall around me like a multicolored curtain.

The mountains are beautiful in the light of day. A multitude of sights, smells and sounds overwhelms my senses. I watch with anticipation as the evening sun disappears slowly beyond the western horizon.

And then there is the night.

Nighttime is a beautiful, benevolent time. The skies sparkle with billions of pinpoints of light, but not enough to stir the life that lies hidden until the sun rises again.

In the darkness, my mind, eyes and ears cannot focus on any given sound or sight. Everything disappears into a mass without distinctive characteristics. All life blends together.

I stand at the foot of the mountain, alone with nature. I close my eyes, and suddenly all my other senses intensify to fill the void. I savor the fragrance of mountain laurel and eastern hemlock. I hear the rustle of crinkled leaves as they fall among the rocks.

Most of all, I feel the coolness of the wind as it blows against me.

I pause for a moment to remember the first time my father brought me here to climb this mountain. I was 12 years old then, and I didn't understand why he humbly raised his hands to the heavens, or why tears filled his eyes. Now I do.

I open my eyes and move forward. Slowly the ground slants upward, challenging me to climb and be king of the mountain. I probably should have brought a light for safety, but that would have been an intrusion.

As the climb becomes steeper, I lean forward to keep my balance. A small branch brushes across my face. Though I stumble over other branches and shallow depressions, I keep pushing myself forward. I know that at the summit, strewn across the sky, stars wait for someone to pay homage.

When at last I reach the top, I pause, take a deep breath and survey God's beautiful domain. I have become king of the mountain, but only I know it. For a brief moment, the mountain, the night and I are one. I'm not the conqueror after all, but one in the presence of something worthy of reverence.

Like my father before me, I find my eyes filling with tears— not from sadness or longing, but from the sheer joy of the life God has given me. Many will never see the wonders I witnessed here, experience the stillness I cherish, or share in the pleasure of climbing to the top of the world to see the awe-inspiring miracles of our creator.

DOUGLAS SCOTT CLARK
MARYVILLE, TENNESSEE

The One-Room Schoolhouse Is Still in Session

IT'S BEEN A WHILE since I've stood with my hand over my heart and said the Pledge of Allegiance. Still, I do pretty well, I think. Then they break into a chorus of "My country 'tis of thee." Six soft, earnest little voices rise up past the flag into that vast Montana sky. By the time they get to "let freedom ring," I have a lump in my throat.

In a world that too often seems to have lost its innocence, these are moments that renew your faith, moments you want to save and cherish forever.

Hunkered in the shadow of the Bridger Mountains 25 miles north of Bozeman, Pass Creek School looks like the classic one-room schoolhouse every country kid in America once attended.

In 1918, there were more than 190,000 one-room country schools in the United States. We have about 400 today, and with fewer than 1 million people spread over 147,000 square miles, Montana accounts for one-fourth. But distance and population density don't really explain why Pass Creek School has survived.

This isn't just a collection of houses; it's a community. The road marker on the corner doesn't point the way to distant towns. It tells you that the Hauglands live 0.3 mile west, the Callantines are 0.5 mile south and Sandy Pew is another 10 miles north.

"About half our students' families have farmed and ranched here for a very long time, and many of their parents went to school here," explains Sid Rider, who's been teaching at Pass Creek for nine years. "They could've given up when the original school burned down in the '50s, but they moved this building down from the mountains and kept going."

Pass Creek has 14 students this year, from kindergarten to eighth grade. We had such an endearingly short crew at the flag raising this morning because the big kids are across the road at band practice in the new community center.

"Before they built that, we held our Christmas pageant in a hog barn," Mrs. Rider notes. The band is polishing up a few songs for eighth-grade graduation next week.

I get the impression that Patty Larios, the band teacher, would like another year or two of practice first. But you have to give the kids credit: All the Pass Creek students from fourth grade on up are here tooting their hearts out.

After the instruments are stashed back at the schoolhouse, Mrs. Rider asks the big kids to stand up and introduce themselves. That would've completely freaked me out when I was in grade school, but it doesn't faze these kids.

As the day goes on, I realize why: Almost everything they do turns into a discussion, group project or performance. "It's hugely social," Mrs. Rider explains. "Everybody's always helping everybody else."

The Massanutten School, Luray, Virginia. PHOTO BY PAT & CHUCK BLACKLEY

Children play during recess (opposite); an eager student raises his hand (below).

PHOTOS BY TERRY WILD

Seems to me they're also noticeably less, well, squirrely, let's say, than a typical roomful of grade-school kids. The younger ones look up to the older ones; the older ones take the responsibility seriously. And they're a lot of fun to be around.

After introductions, the fourth- and fifth-graders settle down to study while the oldest four head for the computers. They're doing online research for their upcoming field trip to Boston.

When the community rebuilt the school in the '50s, they added a lower level, where I now find Lauren Wing, leading her K-through-third-grade kids in a state name song. They're working on the "New" states today.

I'd join in, but I couldn't recite the state names alphabetically if you offered me a million bucks. Instead, I comment that the tune for the "New" states seems to be tripping them up.

"You might be right," Miss Wing agrees, then turns to her third-grader and matter-of-factly asks, "Krista, would you please come up with something better?"

Moments later, Krista raises her hand and says, "I think I've got it." And sure enough, she sings, "New Hampshire, New Jersey, New Mexico, New York" to a new tune that works.

I'd have to stay here a lot longer than a day to catch up with these kids.

Then I head upstairs for biology. We're dissecting frogs to-day, and Abby gets stuck with me as her lab partner. I graciously let her perform the major surgery, but nothing inside here looks anything like the organs in the diagram.

I blame the frog, which could very well be a relic from the last Ice Age. Abby refuses to give up, though, and we eventually find everything but the kidney—or maybe the liver.

After lunch, I decline a gracious invitation to play in their recess soccer game, which turns out to be an alarmingly cutthroat affair with balls and bodies flying around like sheet metal in a tornado. I got a crick in my neck just from dissecting the frog.

After recess, the little kids join the big ones upstairs to share their new words for the day with short stories and funny skits.

The rest of the afternoon flies by, topped off with vocabulary races and scrumptious Mexican wedding cakes.

At one point I ask Dillan, who went to a large grade school before his family moved here, which one he liked better. "Oh, definitely here!" he says, without a moment's hesitation.

He and Catherine will graduate next week and move on to high school. But I suspect they'll always remember the closeness, cooperation and mutual respect that fill this little classroom.

**ROBIN HOFFMAN
TWIN LAKES, WISCONSIN**

A Time of Transition...

Mabry Mill, Blue Ridge Parkway, Virginia.
PHOTO BY PAT & CHUCK BLACKLEY

A Cooper's hawk soars over the Sangre de Cristo Mountains near Santa Fe, New Mexico. PHOTO BY TIM FITZHARRIS

The first touches of autumn decorate these trees in Andover, New Hampshire.

PHOTO BY STEVE TERRILL

Sneffels Range, San Juan Mountains, Colorado.

PHOTO BY LARRY ULRICH

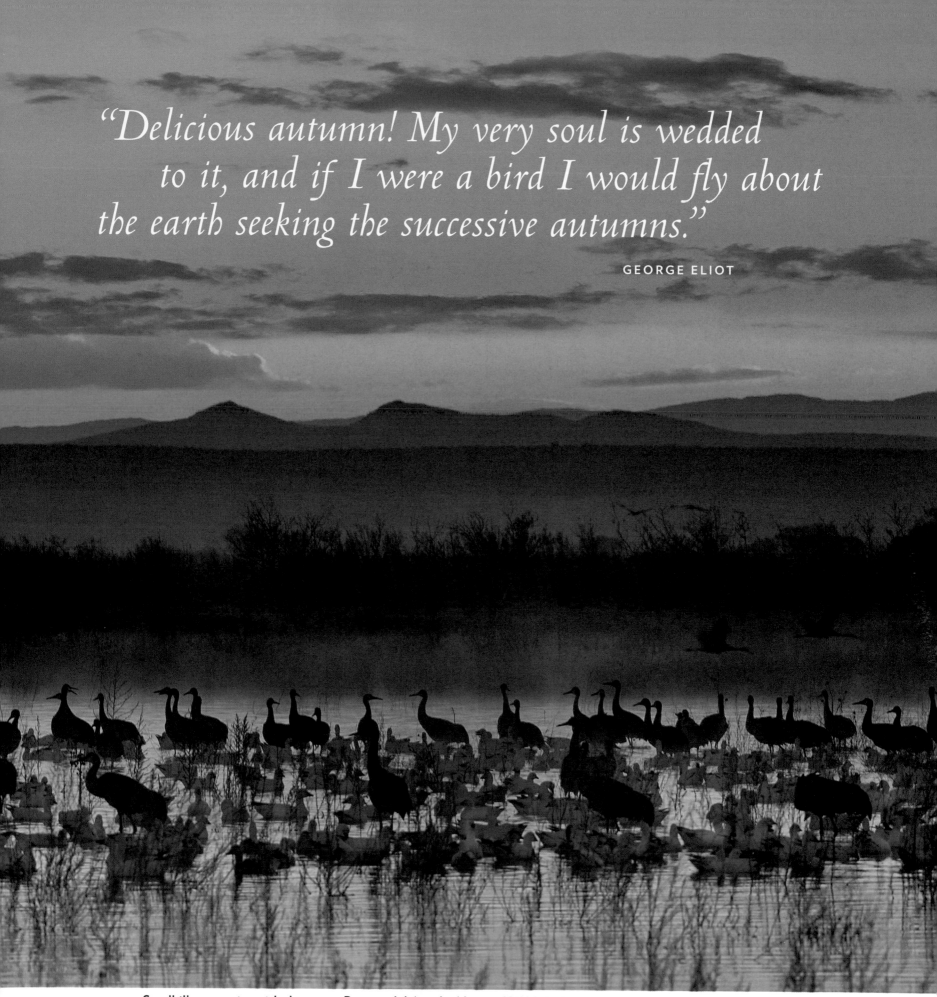

"Delicious autumn! My very soul is wedded to it, and if I were a bird I would fly about the earth seeking the successive autumns."

GEORGE ELIOT

Sandhill cranes rise with the sun in Bosque del Apache National Wildlife Refuge, New Mexico. PHOTO BY TIM FITZHARRIS

101

Old Johnson Farm, Blue Ridge Parkway, Virginia. PHOTO BY PAT & CHUCK BLACKLEY

"The connection between the food we eat and the land was never so clear as around that table."

Grandpa's Place Was Heaven on Earth

GRANDPA LIVED IN A SMALL white farmhouse along a dusty township road on a dozen acres of rolling pasture in Arkansas.

There must have been thousands of farmhouses just like it. But to me, it was like no other place on earth.

When we came to visit, Grandpa waited for us on the porch in his favorite chair. Like Grandpa, the chair was small, sturdy and straightforward. Made of turned oak, it had a woven seat and countless coats of paint. I used to imagine it was brought to the Ozarks on a covered wagon, and for all I know, it was.

From Grandpa's porch, we could see the hazy blue bulge of Boat Mountain on the southern horizon. Beyond lay the wilds of the Boston Mountains.

Grandpa's house was the staging area for many adventures into these mountains, including overnight fishing trips with campfire suppers of fresh bass, hush puppies and wild huckleberry pie.

Suppers were followed by mellow nights with older family members spinning tall tales around the campfire until the embers died, the dew fell and the whippoorwills called from the tops of the pines.

When not camping, we kids slept above the porch in the attic, surrounded by mysterious old trunks and the spicy-sweet scent of drying apples. Moonlight beamed in through the dormer window as giant feather beds almost swallowed us whole. In the fall, dry oak leaves blew against the eaves, and toward morning, frost painted the windowpanes.

For lunch, we'd gather around a large, heavy table with an ancient dark finish that hid the grain. While eating, I could look past the glass honey stand and steaming biscuits across the table and out the window, where I'd see the hive of bees that made the honey and the apple trees where they gathered the nectar.

I could see the cows that provided the butter and the pasture where they grazed. Beyond were the garden that yielded the corn and tomatoes, the smokehouse where the Ozark ham was cured, the ponds that spawned the fish, and the spring where the watercress salad grew just minutes before. The connection between the food we eat and the land was never so clear as around that table—almost everything on it came from within a quarter of a mile of the farmhouse.

The table had another amazing quality—it could seat a seemingly unlimited number. Sometimes it was a bit cramped, and the plates didn't always match. But everyone had a place, and the food somehow multiplied like biblical loaves of bread.

Just before we ate, a spontaneous silence fell across the room, like the calm before a summer rain when the birds hush and the wind dies down. That's when Grandpa offered a simple but eloquent prayer of thanks.

The prayer was always the same, but the sincerity never wavered. Each word was carefully selected, polished and lovingly assembled over Grandpa's 90 years of reverence to God.

As he prayed, I imagined God must have been looking down at the farm and smiling, knowing that in one small corner of a troubled world, all was well.

TERRY DICKEY
WICHITA, KANSAS

"You should have seen those old men. It was like some kind of magic. All of a sudden, they didn't look so old..."

Last of the Boys in Blue

I REMEMBER STANDING in my grandfather's living room, impatiently tapping my foot while the old man finished putting on his army uniform, the one he'd lovingly preserved for more than 70 years.

It was Veterans Day 1968—although the old man still called it Armistice Day—and he was going to be in the parade.

Way back in 1898, my grandfather and his buddies marched off together to "hang the Dons" in our war with Spain. They were the last of the boys in blue—the last soldiers who fought for the United States wearing what they called the "dirty-shirt blue" of the Old Army.

By the fall of 1968, there were only nine of them left in our county, but they were all in fair health and intended to march as a unit, just like they always had. Because they were so few, the WWI veterans had offered to let them march with them, but Papa and his friends refused.

My girlfriend, Sherry, my friend Bobby and I watched as our grandparents made up their own little formation, three columns of three, between the other veterans' formations, our high school marching band and the marching bands from three smaller towns in our county. They were there, on their own, representing their army and their war.

When the men marched onto the square and past the review stand, the band suddenly stopped right in the middle of the march they were playing.

It went completely quiet for a moment. Then the drums, flutes and piccolos began to play *The Girl I Left Behind Me*, the unofficial marching song of the Old Army. Then the three other bands joined in.

You should have seen those old men. It was like some kind of magic. All of a sudden they didn't look so old anymore. They stood a little straighter, a little taller, and for the life of me, the nine of them looked like a regiment passing in review.

We'd never been so proud of our grandparents. For a fleeting instant, we boys saw ourselves in those ranks. We saw ourselves in the faces of the men who had gone before us and given us the names that we bore.

That was the last time they marched. Papa left us in 1982, a few weeks short of 101 years old. He was the last "boy in blue" in our county. I can't tell you how proud I still am of him.

There's an old folk saying that goes something like this, "The only true form of immortality that any of us can hope to have is the time that we live on in the hearts and memories of those who love us and remain behind."

As long as I am able, I will keep the memory of the boys in blue alive in the hearts and minds of my children, my grandchildren and everyone I can reach. As long as I draw breath, the last of the boys in blue will live on.

J. LEE CHORON
CENTER, TEXAS

A U.S. Navy veteran stands with the flag during a ceremony in Hughesville, Pennsylvania (far left); children hold the flag in honor of Veterans Day (left). PHOTOS BY MARK NANCE

Taps stirs the hearts and memories of these men who fought for their country. PHOTO BY MARK NANCE

Our Blessed Country

*A country church sits at the heart of every rural community.
And though the outside may be weathered and worn, the
heart within beats as strong as ever when the faithful
gather to find peace through faith and fellowship.*

Chapel of the Transfiguration, Grand Teton National Park, Wyoming. PHOTO BY TERRY DONNELLY

Immaculate Conception Church, Bastress, Pennsylvania (top).
PHOTO BY TERRY WILD

Methodist Church, McKinley, Virginia (above); English Chapel United Methodist Church, Brevard, North Carolina (left).
PHOTOS BY PAT & CHUCK BLACKLEY

"He was unable to fly, and his lifelong mate would not leave him behind. I marveled at the bond between them."

A Lesson in Devotion

ONE MORNING IN EARLY September, I spotted a pair of wild geese on our pond. The beautiful sight caught me by surprise because we'd never seen geese there before.

I assumed they would soon be on their way, so I savored the opportunity to be close to these graceful creatures. I wondered where they came from and why they'd choosen our pond.

The next morning, the geese were still our guests, so I took a circuitous route to the mailbox to show them I meant no harm.

Still, I couldn't resist getting a closer look. I stopped by some trees near the water's edge and quietly peered through the branches at this beautiful pair. I was surprised to see that the birds were staring back at me!

As the days passed, I started talking to the geese on my trips to the mailbox. They craned their necks and raised their heads cautiously but seemed to realize I was a friend and not a foe. I felt as though we were bonding.

By then, my curiosity about why they were staying so long at the pond changed to concern. It wouldn't be long before the harsh Michigan winter set in and the pond froze over.

One day as they were feeding in the grass near the driveway, I discovered the reason for their visit—the male had a broken left wing. He was unable to fly, and his lifelong mate would not leave him behind. I marveled at the bond between them.

I asked a wildlife biologist friend what I should do. He explained that sometimes a broken wing will heal by itself and suggested letting nature take its course.

Both birds preened themselves daily, but the injured male preened more than the female. I wondered—could this be Mother Nature at work?

On the first day of November, I was working in the vicinity of the geese with my tractor. As I bent to fasten a chain from the tractor to a log I wanted to move, I caught some movement from the corner of my eye. Both geese were running toward the pond, wings beating furiously.

They looked like a couple of B-52s lumbering for takeoff. Gradually, both became airborne and flew over the pond. The geese gained enough altitude to clear a neighbor's house, then circled back toward me, flying no more than 50 feet over my head as if to say goodbye. Then they were out of sight.

The season's first snowflakes fell the very next day. The birds must have sensed that winter was coming and that it was time to go. I grew fond of them during their stay at our pond, and I miss them. I'll never forget their devotion to each other. We could all learn a lesson or two from this pair.

ALLEN BOELTER
BIRCH RUN, MICHIGAN

Canada geese on a pond at dusk. PHOTO BY STEVE TERRILL

Land of Plenty

Spring and summer mean months of work in fields and orchards, but autumn brings the rewards of all that toil. It's time to tuck away the harvest to savor over the winter and give humble thanks for the unmatched bounty of this amazing land.

Playing in the pumpkin patch, San Luis Obispo, California.   PHOTO BY LONDIE GARCIA PADELSKY

Soybean field, Kennedyville, Maryland (above).

PHOTO BY PAT & CHUCK BLACKLEY

Freshly picked corn sits in farm wagons, ready to be brought to the crib, in Lycoming County, Pennsylvania (left).

PHOTO BY TERRY WILD

The Peak of Perfection...

Bigtooth maple and sycamore leaves, South Fork Cave Creek Canyon, Chiricahua Wilderness, Arizona.
PHOTO BY LARRY ULRICH

Near the Dallas Divide, Uncompaghre Mountains, Colorado. PHOTO BY MARY LIZ AUSTIN

Fort Pond, Lancaster, Massachusetts. PHOTO BY PAUL REZENDES

"*Winter is an etching, spring a watercolor,
summer an oil painting and
autumn a mosaic of them all.*"

STANLEY HOROWITZ

Blueberry fields, Amherst, Maine. PHOTO BY PAUL REZENDES

**Cliffs of Chapel Rock, Pictured Rocks
National Lakeshore, Lake Superior, Michigan.**

PHOTO BY TERRY DONNELLY

Winter moonrise in Putnam County, Illinois.
PHOTO BY TERRY DONNELLY

Winter
The Land at Peace

"It was in those moments that I understood teamwork, encouragement and what it means to be a finisher."

Lessons From the Woodpile

I HAVE ALWAYS LOVED being outside, and I spent most of my childhood in the woods behind our house. There, my sister, Amy, and my brother, Adam, and I whiled away our free time. With rocks, trees and lots of imagination, we created the most amazing places—houses full of rooms, secure forts, secret hideouts, and once even a wild animal preserve.

But being outside sometimes meant being put to work. In the winter, I could always count on Dad tracking me down to help him go "up on the hill" for a load of firewood.

I put on my snowsuit, mismatched mittens crocheted by Grandma—one too small and one too big, or two "lefties"—and an orange stocking hat that should have been worn for hunting. I was an embarrassing sight, to be sure. But I was warm, and if my similarly clad siblings went along, I looked almost normal.

We climbed into Dad's homemade red wagon behind his old John Deere B. The putt-putt of the engine resounded in our ears, and the great black tires and the clanking chains that hung on them mesmerized us as we watched them go round and round. We finally arrived at a remote destination, after bumping over a road that was called that only because someone had the courage and determination to drive there once before.

The air was fresh and crisp—like it had been born just that morning. Upon our arrival, the scolding of a disgruntled blue jay and the echo of Dad's ax coming down squarely into a chunk of stubborn hardwood were about the only sounds until Dad's chain saw roared to life.

The chain saw spit yellow, fragrant sawdust over the top of the snow, and the scent of it became the scent of Dad. At those moments, he was the strongest, hardest-working and smartest man in my childhood universe. He never complained or tired. He just worked because that was what had to be done.

One piece of firewood at a time, I piled our winter fuel into Dad's wagon. I did not want to be there. This was work. Slowly, my grumpiness faded as the wagon reached quarter full. Our progress gave me a glimmer of hope that we'd finish before I was 20, a feat that seemed impossible to my 11-year-old mind just a half hour earlier.

Amy, Adam and I developed all kinds of strategies and games for filling the last few feet of the wagon. It was in those moments that I understood teamwork, encouragement and what it means to be a finisher.

I didn't realize then the significance of the lessons I was learning in that outdoor classroom. I only knew the incredible feeling of accomplishment I had as I triumphantly rode down off the hill atop that wagonload of wood, pulled by Dad, my hero, and riding next to Adam and Amy, my teammates.

I had won—and together we had been successful. In spite of my initial reluctance, I had persevered and stepped up to the task at hand.

Now, as I think about those mornings in the woods, something long-dormant stirs within me. I will always cherish the outdoors, in part because of its beauty, but also because of the life lessons I learned there in the woods. I draw on knowledge gained at the woodpile as I go about my duties as a sixth-grade teacher and girls' high school basketball coach.

Every day, I hope to find a few seeming impossibilities like Dad's empty wood wagon and overcome them. I want to pass those lessons on to the many children who watch me closely from their desks to see what I will do. The same goes for the girls who call me "Coach."

That way, at the end of each day, I put my last log atop that mountain of firewood and climb aboard the wagon for home. In so doing, I recapture the feel of dirty, wet mittens, the scent of fresh-cut firewood, the sight of a brimming wagon, and the memory of my dad's silent but sure pride in what we had learned and accomplished together as a family.

ERIN HILLS
POUGHKEEPSIE, NEW YORK

A trusty '52 Ford awaits its next job near Royalston, Massachusetts. PHOTO BY PAUL REZENDES

Winter Wash Days

WE ALWAYS had a good time together doing laundry in winter during the 1920s.

Just getting the water ready was fun. See, after a big snowstorm, my father used a big grain shovel to cut out huge slabs of snow.

We kids helped carry the slabs into the house. Sometimes we threw the slabs at each other. The slabs would break into small pieces and we'd break into laughter. Then Pa would have to go out and cut more.

We dumped the slabs into an empty 50-gallon vinegar barrel and poured kettles of boiling water over the snow to melt it. Then we got Mother's glass rub board and took turns doing the hard part of the wash.

The clothes were hung outdoors on a long clothesline. When they didn't dry before sundown, we carried them in, frozen stiff. Then my sister and I waltzed around the kitchen with the frozen long johns. Our parents laughed and laughed. When the underwear thawed, we dashed outdoors to fetch another garment from the line and repeat our performance.

Yes, winter wash days were definitely more fun when I was a carefree teenager!

MILLY OSVOLD WELLS
ENGLEWOOD, COLORADO

Freeze-dried laundry in Holmes County, Ohio. PHOTO BY DOYLE YODER

Warm Memories of a Woodstove

LARGE FLUFFY SNOWFLAKES had fallen all afternoon, so after supper I decided to go for a walk in the new snow to quiet myself from the day's worries.

I noticed smoke curling from the chimney of the house across the street, and the scent of the burning wood mixed with the cold night air brought back memories of the years I lived on a small farm in Nebraska. There I discovered the pleasures of burning firewood in a woodstove.

Occasionally I'd burn wood in the fireplace and daydream as I watched the flickering flames. But much of the heat went up the chimney, so most of the time, I fired up the woodstove. It was more efficient and radiated warmth throughout the house.

On snowy days when I came in from the cold with dripping boots and soaked gloves, I pulled a chair close, but not too close, to the ol' woodstove and let my wet clothes and boots dry.

Sometimes, in the evenings, I'd get a fire going and curl up on the couch with a cup of coffee and a good book. The old stove creaked and cracked as it heated up, and later, as it cooled down, it would make similar noises.

My dogs, Rag and Tag, followed my example and curled up on the kitchen floor. Every so often I'd get up from the couch, add wood to the stove, look out the kitchen window to check the thermometer and refill my coffee cup.

As if on cue, Rag and Tag would also stand, stretch and circle, then scratch the rug and again curl up into tight balls on the floor. Occasionally one of them would let out a soft yelp and squirm about—probably chasing a rabbit or a squirrel in her dreams.

Sometimes I'd fall asleep on the couch enjoying the warmth and quiet of the evening. Eventually, the room began to chill, and I'd awaken, knowing that the stove was hungry again.

I miss those special times on the farm and the simple pleasures that I had. Whenever I get a whiff of wood smoke in the cold air, it rekindles warm memories of long winter evenings in the country with my dogs and my woodstove.

PETE GEPSON
DUNLAP, IOWA

A woodpile promises winter warmth (above), while skaters in Lycoming County, Pennsylvania (top), enjoy the cold.

PHOTOS BY TERRY WILD

Cozy cabin in Okanogan County, Washington. PHOTO BY TERRY DONNELLY

Travelers in the Storm...

Gray wolves. PHOTO BY TIM FITZHARRIS

Amish buggies brave a snowy country road near Fredericksburg, Ohio. PHOTO BY DOYLE YODER

Bison search for a meal under the snow in Wyoming's Yellowstone National Park. PHOTO BY TIM FITZHARRIS

"Everybody needs beauty as well as bread, places to play in and pray in, where nature may heal and give strength to body and soul."

JOHN MUIR

Riding the range in California's Eastern Sierra. PHOTO BY LONDIE GARCIA PADELSKY

"Several times, he slipped to his knees. But he always scrambled up and kept on, legs scraped and bloody from the sharp ice."

Their Last Hope Was a Horse Named Duke

"HAVE DOC COME right away!" our neighbor Doris yelled through the phone line. "Suzie fell through the ice!" Suzie was a half-Arabian mare that Doris had raised from a colt.

Everyone called my father Doc. He was an old-time country veterinarian for the small dairy farms that still flourished in New England 50 years ago. I joined him on house calls.

Within minutes, we were on our way, bags of electrolyte sloshing around in a pail of piping hot water. As Doc sped up the hill to Doris' house, I began toweling off the bags so I could carry them under my coat and keep them warm.

Doc and a couple of the other hands pulled Suzie to shore. Suzie had been fighting to get out when the men found her. But she'd gotten weaker the longer she floundered in the icy water.

Now, she lay on the snowy shore in hypothermic shock, motionless and slicked with ice. Doc pulled a stethoscope from his jacket and listened to Suzie's heart and respiration.

"Gather wood and get some fires going around her," he finally said. "Hurry! We're losing ground fast."

Then he told me, "We've got to get warm electrolytes in her to bring up her core temperature." We felt a little better when he got the IV going, then the fluid began to freeze in the tube. We built a fire under the tube, but it was only a temporary fix.

The weak January sun was slipping below the horizon and the temperature plummeted below zero. We had to get Suzie to a warm place, but no truck or tractor could make it down the steep, narrow horse path.

Suzie was catatonic. Then Doris whispered, "She's in foal."

"Do you have a neighbor with a team of draft horses that could pull Suzie up on a skidder?" Doc asked.

"No," Doris sobbed. "Warren Jenks has one old half-bred, but I don't think he's nearly strong enough to haul Suzie up this hill."

"Go call Warren," Doc said. "We'll have to find out."

I kept rubbing Suzie's limp legs with an old blanket. A half-hour later, we saw the flicker of a distant lantern. Warren and his horse Duke had come to help. Duke was a scraggly old draft horse with long chestnut hair. And he was small. Way too small. My eyes welled with tears as the sad-looking horse plodded by.

"Evening, Doc, Miss, boys," Warren said, as the skidder rested next to Suzie. "I see Duke has his work cut out for 'im."

"You think he can do it?" I asked. Warren could surely tell I didn't think so, but he didn't let on.

"Don't really know for sure, Miss. But he's strong and clever 'bout things. He'll do his best; that I know."

We rolled Suzie onto the skidder. Then I walked to where Duke could see me. His big brown eyes peered into mine. "Can you do it, Duke?" I asked.

I can't say he answered me, exactly. But when the steamy whiskers of his muzzle brushed against my cold cheek, I believed he understood the task he faced.

As the old horse leaned into the harness, the skidder broke loose with a sound like shattering glass. With its ungainly load, the skidder kept tipping and hanging up on the icy, curving path. Duke was forced to make his own way through deep, ice-crusted snow—step by treacherous step.

Several times, he slipped to his knees. But he always scrambled up and kept on, legs scraped and bloody from the sharp ice.

Duke's flanks broke out in white, lathering sweat. Steam rose from his back and hung over him like a shroud. His breath ripped through the frigid air in loud, raspy gasps. This job would wear down a team of young draft horses. Still, Duke pulled on, his hindquarters quivering with every step to the barn door.

As the men dragged Suzie into the warm barn, I took care of Duke. Sweat ran down his heaving flanks and poured like rain from his belly. Someone threw me a blanket to drape over him. I found a cloth to wipe his face.

As I looked once again into those placid brown eyes, I asked, "Do you know what you just did?" Somehow, I think he knew.

Suzie lived and gave birth to a healthy bay colt. Tough stock, I'd say. I never saw Duke again. But to this day, I can close my eyes and see the steam rising from his flanks. I can feel his relentless determination and know the comfort of looking into eyes that say, "I'll do my best," and mean it.

CAROLYN MILLS-MEYER
SOUTHBRIDGE, MASSACHUSETTS

A good draft horse lives to work, no matter the weather. PHOTO BY DOYLE YODER

Dinnertime in western Highland County, Virginia. PHOTO BY PAT & CHUCK BLACKLEY

"The barns didn't seem so far away now. I noticed how the sun made the snow sparkle and glisten as I listened to the wonderful sounds of a cow's tongue washing a warm, contented calf."

A Job Well Done

A FOOT OF SNOW on a bright, clear February morning is a beautiful sight unless you're a rancher with calving cows.

If that's the case, you tend to forget about beauty and wish you and your cows were a couple hundred miles south. That's how I felt one crisp February morning a few years ago.

On this particularly cold, frosty morning, I started out by loading a bale of hay on our old Chevy truck and heading out to give the cows their breakfast.

The night before, I'd noticed that two ol' gals seemed ready to drop their calves. Today, one of them came up with the herd, but the other was nowhere in sight. I checked all the usual spots and still couldn't find her.

I headed up a hill and, sure enough, from the top, I could see the heifer standing in a brush line, as far away from our barns as she could be. From the way she was standing, I figured she'd had her calf. She seemed to be OK.

When I got closer, I saw a big, fine calf tucked next to an old hedge tree. He was cold and shaking. He hadn't been up yet and sure needed a meal. I got a couple of burlap bags from the truck and rubbed him to get his circulation going, but he couldn't stand; his big-boned, knobby-kneed legs wouldn't hold him.

I had to warm this calf up. I looked back at the barns; they seemed a thousand miles away. The truck's heater was broken, so I couldn't warm him up in the cab.

All that calf needed was a little bit of his mama's milk. Studying the heifer, I got an idea. I had a sack of sweet feed in the truck, so I got a pail and shook some out in the hay where she was eating.

Then I carried the calf closer to his mama. She watched me but didn't move away. About 2 feet away, I draped him over my knee and started inching him toward her udder.

She occasionally swung her head around to watch us but didn't move or kick. I stretched the calf's neck out and put his mouth against her udder—still no reaction.

I gently touched her udder. She didn't kick the blue blazes out of me, so I got bolder. I opened the calf's mouth and milked a bit of colostrum into his mouth, then rubbed his throat.

After about five minutes, his little tail suddenly twitched and he began to look interested. I moved him closer, and he got down to business. In a few more minutes, I realized I was no longer supporting his entire weight.

I inched back, relieved to get some distance between me and the kicking end of the cow. The calf got a belly full, then nestled down in a pile of hay. Mama finished up her eating, then gave baby a few good licks.

As I stood there, my jeans—wet from the calf and the snow—began to freeze and stiffen. But I had the warmest glow inside of me that I'd ever felt on a February morning.

As I looked around, the barns didn't seem so far away now. I noticed how the sun made the snow sparkle and glisten as I listened to the wonderful sound of a cow's tongue washing a warm, contented calf. It was a good morning on the ranch.

NORA POWELL
STOCKTON, MISSOURI

Heart of the Farm

There's no place on the farm more cherished than the barn. Within those weathered walls, a family's future is forged. Children who follow their parents to the barn learn the value of hard work and a deep, enduring respect for life on the land.

A grand old bank barn in Sharon, Connecticut. PHOTO BY PAUL REZENDES

A snug horse barn in Brightwood, Oregon (above).
PHOTO BY STEVE TERRILL

Classic gambrel-roofed Vermont dairy barn (top).
PHOTO BY TERRY WILD

Round barn in Henry County, Illinois. PHOTO BY MARY LIZ AUSTIN

> *"My character was formed in the barn. It's where I was schooled in the values and lessons of life."*
>
> MARLA BRAFF, HURLEY, WISCONSIN

Thanks to a barn full of hay, these horses can enjoy a brisk snowstorm in Wallowa County, Oregon. PHOTO BY DAVID JENSEN

> *"After dinner, we traded homemade scarves, caps and Christmas candy. It was simple. It was about belonging. It was love."*

The More the Merrier

OUR NEIGHBOR JOHN BURNS stood with his head down and a worn suitcase in each hand. A boy with brown eyes and dark hair stood to his right, and a fair-haired girl stood to his left.

"Wait, and I'll get Ron," I said.

A few minutes later, I found my husband out back pruning apple trees in the December chill. "John Burns is at the door. You better come."

When we returned, John said, "I just went through a very bad divorce. I lost my job. And I seriously don't know what to do."

He paused and cleared his throat before forging ahead. "I was wondering if you would take Brian and Amy. I don't want them to end up in foster care again, and I couldn't help noticing your kids seem real happy."

In the silence that followed, John stared down at the ground. His children's big, sad eyes were glued on my husband's.

It was three weeks before Christmas 1980. Oregon was in yet another recession, and this man wasn't the only one who'd lost his job. Ron had been laid off just before Thanksgiving.

"Well, I sure don't see why not," Ron finally replied.

I felt like someone was standing on my chest. My heart pounded in my ears, but I didn't say a word.

After we finally got everyone in bed that night, I lay awake listening to the winter wind blow across our mountain. I thought about the bear that came twice a year when the prunes were ripe. I thought about the double rainbows we often saw stretched across our orchard after a rain and how much I loved this place.

Then my thoughts turned to this unsettling day. My mind raced with questions I couldn't answer.

Beside me, Ron snored peacefully in the darkness. He was a worker, not a worrier. He got up before dawn to care for our sheep or to work in the orchard before going off to haul mobile homes (when there were mobile homes to haul). When he got home at night, he'd eat a quick supper, then go off to fix fences, haul hay or repair equipment.

But the man always found time for his children. And regardless of whatever else you could say about John Burns, he had made a wise choice in asking Ron to take care of his kids.

The short days of December raced toward Christmas. Our three children—Nanci, 12; Randy, 11; and Melodie, 10—faced many adjustments, sharing rooms, beds, clothes, toys and parents. They made the best of it, though, and we were very proud of them.

My mother always remembered us at Christmas, and her package arrived from Anchorage, Alaska, in mid-December. I opened the box and rewrapped the presents, making five out of three.

I called Ron's mother in Albany, about 40 miles away, to tell her we'd be bringing five children to her house for Christmas this year. She chuckled kindheartedly and said that would be just fine. The apple didn't fall far from the tree in that family.

On Christmas Day, Ron's brother, Doug, met us at the door of their parents' old farmhouse with a jolly, "Merry Christmas!" Inside, we were greeted with the cozy warmth of a woodstove, big hugs and laughter. Ron's family made everyone feel welcome.

After dinner, we traded homemade scarves, caps and Christmas candy. Each child got a small toy. Ron's dad insisted Janet and Carol, the youngest aunts, lead the Christmas carols while Mom Roth accompanied us on her old upright piano.

It was simple. It was about belonging. It was love.

All five kids fell asleep on the long drive home. As we turned onto the road to our small farm on Rainbow Mountain, snow fell in flakes so thick they sliced the beam of the car's headlights like a curtain. Ron stopped to enjoy the beautiful, peaceful sight.

"That's all I wanted for Christmas!" Randy suddenly exclaimed from the backseat. "Tomorrow we can get the old toboggan out of the barn. I hope it snows all night!"

I was hoping the water pipes in the house didn't freeze, when a tear slid down my cheek. Why couldn't we give our children nice Christmas gifts like bicycles and new sleds? It wasn't fair. Just then, two little arms went around my neck, and Nanci whispered in my ear, "I love you, Mom."

Brian and Amy were now awake and looking over the front seat as Melodie sang, "We wish you a merry Christmas." All the children joined in. Ron's eyes met mine, and he gave me a smile I'll never forget. Then we continued up our mountain, leaving fresh tracks in the new-fallen snow.

MADISON ROTHCHILD
DALLAS, OREGON

Holiday lights warm a snowy fencerow in Bureau County, Illinois. PHOTO BY TERRY DONNELLY

Cows as fat and sassy as these Herefords don't mind a little snow. PHOTO BY DAVID JENSEN

The Cows Don't Know It's Christmas

Today's the day we celebrate
Our Savior's birth; a special date.
We'll go to church, but we'll be late,
'Cause the cows don't know it's Christmas.

It's cold outside and frosty, too.
I've got some Christmas things to do,
But I can't stop; I hear 'em moo.
The cows don't know it's Christmas.

The kids are anxious, dancin' round;
They want to get their stockings down.
I'd like to help; I see them frown.
But the cows don't know it's Christmas.

The rooster's up; I heard him crow.
The geese are walking in a row.
I'd like to stay in bed, but no…
The cows don't know it's Christmas.

The baby lambs, they're layin' down.
"Too cold for us," they seem to frown.
My baby girl's still in her gown.
But the cows don't know it's Christmas.

I've got to go down to the barn.
To all the world, it's a special morn,
But each day's the same here at the farm,
'Cause the cows don't know it's Christmas.

I'll bust the bales and drop them down
(All's left are th' square…done fed the round).
And soon enough, we'll go to town,
But the cows don't know it's Christmas.

You gotta wonder 'bout it all;
So long ago, in that manger stall,
When they heard the Baby Jesus bawl,
And the cows did know…it's Christmas!

STEVE CHERRY
DENISON, TEXAS

Let It Snow...

Peaceful scene near Swoope, Virginia.
PHOTO BY PAT & CHUCK BLACKLEY

Frosty fun at Frease Road School in Wayne County, Ohio. PHOTO BY DOYLE YODER

"*I love snow for the same reason I love Christmas: It brings people together while time stands still.*"
RACHEL COHN

Teton Range from Snake River Overlook, Grand Teton National Park, Wyoming. PHOTO BY TIM FITZHARRIS

"I've often wondered if Herbert and his family were angels sent to help us understand the spirit of Christmas."

The Best Gift I Ever Gave — or Got

THE WINTER WIND WHISTLED across the West Texas plains. Tumbleweeds drifted into our barbed-wire fence, and laundry froze stiff on the line. Christmas 1944 was just days away, and I hoped a deep snow would come with it.

One morning, my brother, Bobby, and I stepped outside and watched a battered truck pull up beside the rundown house at the end of the road. Kids piled out and scattered across the yard, moving too fast to count.

After lunch, I heard someone in the backyard. It was one of the new kids, and he was on my red scooter. I tried to be nice, because I knew Mother was watching me, but I didn't want him on that scooter.

The boy's name was Herbert, and he wanted to know if we had anything else to play with. Bobby picked up a baseball and asked if he wanted to play catch. Herbert threw down my scooter, and I quickly escaped down the road with it.

On top of that, we still didn't have a Christmas tree, and Mother had just told us we weren't going to my grandparents' this year. My father had only one day off, and we didn't have enough time or money for the trip.

No family at Christmas! No Grandmother to hug me and fix my favorite food. No Granddaddy to dance his jig and make us laugh. No aunts, uncles or cousins. It would be the first Christmas I could remember without family. I didn't say much, but I wanted to cry. The howling wind just made it worse.

The next day, Herbert and two of his brothers were in our yard again. Mother made sugar cookies and those boys gobbled them down as if they'd never eaten cookies before.

While we sat on the doorstep, I mentioned that Santa Claus was coming on Saturday. Herbert munched his sugar cookie and matter-of-factly told us Santa had never been to his house. I felt so terrible I didn't know what to say.

At supper, I told Mother what Herbert had said. She looked at my dad, and I saw the sadness in her eyes. My father told us Santa might have had trouble finding Herbert's family because they probably moved a lot.

The next morning, Mother rushed off to see Mrs. Phillips and Mrs. Palmer. They were planning something.

When Daddy got home, Mother told us we were going to do something to help Herbert's family. It had to be a secret; we couldn't talk about it all, not even with our friends.

We had no money to buy gifts, so Mother asked us to make or find something to give the children. The Phillips and Palmer families would do the same.

We didn't have many store-bought toys. That night, my mind churned as I tried to think of the perfect gift. When I came up with an idea, I really wished I hadn't.

I liked my scooter better than anything I had. It wasn't new when I got it, but I thought it was the best scooter in the world because Aunt Winnie had given it to me. I tossed and turned, trying to make up my mind.

The next morning, I told my parents I wanted to give Herbert my scooter. They looked surprised. "Are you sure?" my father asked. I was. Daddy suggested I paint it a different color so Herbert wouldn't recognize it. That night, he brought home a can of pretty blue paint and a little bell for the handlebars.

After we painted the scooter, Bobby got his baseball from his bedroom and wrote "Babe Ruth" on it in black crayon so Herbert wouldn't know it had been his. It must have been as hard for him to give up that beat-up ball as it was for me to give away my scooter. He and J.C. Phillips played a lot of catch.

The lump in my throat was so big I could hardly swallow. I wanted to hug Bobby, but I figured he'd kick me in the shin.

After supper on Christmas Eve, we walked down to the Palmers' with our gifts for Herbert's family. The Phillips family was already there. It was like a grand, happy party.

As we walked home, quietly holding hands, a million stars twinkled in the clear black sky. The Christmas star seemed to shine right down on us.

Overnight, we got about a foot of snow. Big flakes were still fluttering down when Daddy and I sneaked over to where we could see Herbert's porch without him seeing us. Herbert was yelling, "He came! He came!" I blinked back tears. Daddy took my hand, and we walked back to our little house.

I've often wondered if Herbert and his family were angels sent to help us understand the spirit of Christmas. Our gifts were small, but our hearts were true, and the Lord poured out his blessings in a way I will never forget.

CLAUDIA GRISHAM
SPRING, TEXAS

Chihuahuan Desert prickly pear cactus in Big Bend National Park, Texas. PHOTO BY TOM ALGIRE

Holiday lights in Leavenworth, Washington.   PHOTO BY MARY LIZ AUSTIN

"Tears came to my eyes, and, for a moment, I let myself imagine brightly wrapped presents under our Christmas tree."

Kindness of Silence

I'D GIVEN UP HOPE of buying presents for our children the Christmas of 1956. My husband was going to college and working part time. His small salary barely paid for the rent.

I kept telling myself the children were too young to understand what gifts were. Our son was not yet 2 years old, and our baby daughter was only 3 months.

But I understood, and it broke my heart that we couldn't afford toys. A Christmas tree was all our small budget could bear.

On Christmas Eve it began to snow, and there were hardly any cars on the roads. So I was surprised when I heard the stomping of feet on our front porch.

"Mom! Dad! What are you doing out on a night like this?" I asked as I opened the door.

Dad brushed off some snow and reached into his pocket for his wallet. Mom just smiled as he pulled out $25.

"I got an unexpected bonus at work today," Dad explained. "We've done our Christmas shopping and don't need this."

Didn't need it? Mom and Dad's farm was too small to support them, so Dad had been forced to take a job at a factory. Of course they could use this Christmas windfall.

Dad held the money toward me. "We want you to have it. You can buy something for the kids," he insisted.

Tears came to my eyes, and, for a moment, I let myself imagine brightly wrapped presents under our Christmas tree. Then I remembered, "It's already Christmas Eve. All of the stores have probably closed by now."

Dad seemed to have all the answers that night. "I saw an ad in the paper," he said. "There's an auction in town."

"An auction? On Christmas Eve? Who would hold an auction tonight, and what would they be selling?" I wondered.

Dad shrugged. "I don't know what they have. It just said, 'All new merchandise.' Maybe there'll be something for the kids."

Still doubtful, I put on my coat and followed Dad out into the snow. The unplowed roads made our trip to town slow, but we eventually found the place listed in the ad.

It was an empty store on a small side street. Through the lighted window, we saw a small group had gathered in the unheated building, their collars turned up and shoulders hunched.

As we entered, I heard the auctioneer's chant. I glanced around at the merchandise and spotted several toys. In fact, the next item up was a set of toy pots and pans.

Quickly, I called out, "One dollar." Another person raised it by 50¢. I went to $2 and the pans were mine.

Soon a child-sized table with two matching chairs came up for sale. Again, I opened the bidding with $1.

The set was so cute that two other people also bid. But I didn't give up—this was something that would last the children for years. Eventually my $5 bid won, and I began to smile.

Noticing my happiness, the auctioneer said, "Looks like someone is doing some last-minute Christmas shopping."

Then he held up a doll. "Is this something you could use?"

I knew my daughter would be old enough for her first doll in a few months, so I anxiously nodded my head.

"You bidding $1?" the auctioneer asked with a grin. I nodded.

He glanced quickly around the room, pounded his gavel before anyone could get in another bid and said, "Seems no one else is interested. Sold for $1 to the young lady."

And so it went. Whenever a toy came up, the auctioneer turned to me for my $1 bid. "Do I hear another bid?" he'd ask.

Country folks catch on fast, and no one bid against me. So by the end of the evening, I had bought the small table and chairs, the toy pots and pans, the doll, a rocking horse, teddy bear and a set of play dishes. And I still had $13 left in my pocket!

Growing up on a farm, I was used to country folks not being talkative. But never had country love spoken louder than that night when my $1 bids were met with silence.

NANCY UNO
LOTUS, CALIFORNIA

149

A Sacred Stillness...

Frozen waterfall in Starved Rock State Park, Illinois.

PHOTO BY TERRY DONNELLY

The sun sets on Wizard Island in Oregon's Crater Lake National Park. PHOTO BY STEVE TERRILL

Merced River below El Capitan in California's Yosemite National Park.
PHOTO BY LARRY ULRICH

Mount Hood National Forest, Oregon.
PHOTO BY STEVE TERRILL

Contributing Photographers

MARY LIZ AUSTIN

Mary Liz Austin is a professional landscape photographer who strives to create an intimate relationship with her subject, whether it's a grand landscape or a nature portrait. She travels the United States searching for scenes that depict quintessential Americana and the magnificence and distinctive beauty of our national lands. She is proficient in both large-format and digital media, and her work is featured in countless books, calendars and magazines. Her images and stories have graced the pages of *Country* magazine for 15 years. Mary Liz lives on Vashon Island, Washington, with her husband, photographer Terry Donnelly.

PAT & CHUCK BLACKLEY

Pat and Chuck Blackley are a photography and writing team born and raised in Virginia. Although they work throughout North America, their concentration is on the eastern United States. With a love of history, they find a wealth of subjects throughout the mid-Atlantic, particularly in Virginia. The National Parks Conservation Association has described them as among "America's most accomplished conservation photographers." Their books include *Shenandoah National Park Impressions*, *Blue Ridge Parkway Impressions*, *Shenandoah Valley Impressions*, *Outer Banks Impressions*, *Backroads From the Beltway*, *Our Virginia*, *Blue Ridge Parkway Simply Beautiful* and *Virginia's Historic Homes and Gardens*.

TERRY DONNELLY

Terry Donnelly is an award-winning landscape and nature photographer whose images have appeared in Reiman Media Group publications, including *Country*, since 1988. "My greatest joy in photography is in engaging the challenge of interpreting the beauty of nature in new, meaningful ways." Terry's photography has been featured by many prominent publishers of books, magazines and calendars, and he has six large-format books to his credit. He also enjoys teaching photography and leading workshops in Yellowstone National Park and on Vashon Island, Washington. He lives and works with his wife, Mary Liz Austin, on Vashon Island.

TIM FITZHARRIS

Well known to North American photographers through his regular nature column in *Popular Photography & Imaging* magazine, Tim Fitzharris is author and photographer of 30 books on wilderness and wildlife, including *Nature Photography: National Audubon Society Guide*, *Rocky Mountains* and, most recently, *Big Sky*. Featured exclusively in more than 100 landscape calendars, his work is published worldwide, appearing on the covers of *Life*, *Audubon*, *Nature's Best*, *Terre Sauvage* and numerous other leading periodicals. He lives with his wife and two children in Santa Fe, New Mexico.

LONDIE GARCIA PADELSKY

A native Californian born into a ranching family in San Luis Obispo, Londie Garcia Padelsky is an outdoor adventure photographer who has lived at the base of the Eastern Sierra Mountains for almost 30 years.

One of Londie's first photo essays for *Country* was called "God's Country: The Sierra Nevada." It was published in 1993. Since then she has shared numerous stories and photos, from treasured moments with family and country friends to wild adventures such as horsepacking trips in the high country, rugged cowboy cattle roundups, and kayaking trips around the pristine Alaskan islands. Londie has two pictorial books: *California Missions* and *Outhouses: Flushing Out America's Hidden Treasures*. See more of Londie's photography at *londie.com*.

PAUL REZENDES

Inspired by his lifelong love for nature, Paul Rezendes specializes in medium, large-format and digital North American landscapes and seascapes, with a special emphasis on his native New England. Each year, his photographs are featured in hundreds of books, magazines and calendars, including *Tracking & the Art of Seeing, The Wild Within, Martha's Vineyard Seasons, Massachusetts Impressions* and the *Lighthouse Companion Guide* series. Paul also accepts photo assignments and offers fine art prints for sale at *paulrezendes.com*. Paul lives with his wife in a remote forest on the Millers River in Athol, Massachusetts. He has been a contributing photographer to *Country* for 21 years.

STEVE TERRILL

Steve Terrill was born and raised and still makes his home in Portland, Oregon. His work has appeared in Reiman publications since the mid-1980s, and he was one of the original field editors for *Country* magazine. His work has been featured in numerous places, including National Geographic publications and *Travel & Leisure, Outdoor Photographer* and *Sunset* magazines. His images have been used in advertising for such clients as Nike, Honda, Kodak, Nikon and Hewlett-Packard. Steve's photos have been displayed at the White House and by the Smithsonian. He has more than 20 books to his credit.

LARRY ULRICH

Larry Ulrich has been making a living with a sharp eye for the beauty and soul of this country for 40 years, first with a 4x5 film camera and now with a digital Nikon system. He and his wife, Donna, have worked as field editors for *Country* magazine for a good portion of that time, Larry with his photos and Donna with her words. They run a little agency, marketing to such icons as the Sierra Club, Audubon and National Geographic, and have taken enough calendar shots to fill the Grand Canyon. Larry and Donna live in Trinidad, on California's north coast.

TERRY WILD

A full-time photographer since 1974, Terry Wild lives and works in central Pennsylvania. His work is known internationally, and he has been published in countless magazines and calendars. Terry, one of the founders of the Eagles Mere Art Gallery, concentrates on continuing to build his online picture stock library, *www.terrywild stock.com*. His work spans a variety of concentrations, but his emphasis is on agricultural subjects and landscapes as well as country life, flora and fauna.

DOYLE YODER

Born in 1957 and raised in the quiet countryside of New Bedford, Ohio, Doyle Yoder captures beautiful scenes of Amish country life in Holmes and surrounding counties and across the United States. He always strives to be respectful of the Amish, and has a talent for being in the right place at the right time to capture special scenes. In addition to photography, Doyle has many different ventures, including local business advertising, pre-press publishing, co-writing books and publishing his famous *Amish Country* calendars, postcards and puzzles.

Guest photographers include Tom Algire, Gary Alan Nelson, Chuck Haney, Robert Dawson, David Jensen, Jeff Vanuga, Cathy and Gordon Illg, William H. Johnson, David Shaw and Mark Nance.

This heart-shaped grove graces a vineyard on California's central coast. PHOTO BY LONDIE GARCIA PADELSKY

Why I Love *Country*

WITH NO HELP from either of our families, my husband, Clifford, and I took out a small loan to start our farm almost 60 years ago. We pulled ourselves up by our own bootstraps, and once that money was paid off we never had to borrow again.

We lived through some tough times, but we managed to raise three children. We never had the money to spend on vacations, so *Country* magazine has been our window on this great land.

Though I wouldn't trade my life as a farmer's wife for anything, I have been envious at times of others who can travel. But all in all, I am satisfied with my life as a country girl in these great old United States of America.

Clifford and I are now retired and live in a small Iowa town. We are always glad for a reason to get out and drive through the countryside to see that growing crops and tidy farmsteads are still a part of this great country.

Country has been good to us.

MARGARET HULL
AGENCY, IOWA

Swift Diamond River, New Hampshire.

*"Gratitude is the fairest blossom
which springs from the soul."*

HENRY WARD BEECHER

"The biggest sunflower I ever did see!" near San Luis Obispo, California. PHOTO BY LONDIE GARCIA PADELSKY